YOUR SOUL IS CALLING YOU

Inspirational past life regression stories.

Valarie Coventry
Bachelor of Applied Science – Psychology
Diplomas – Hypnotherapy & Regression therapy

Copyright © 2012

All rights reserved. No part of this book may be used or reproduced by any means, graphic, electronic, or mechanical, including photocopying, recording, taping or by any information storage retrieval system without the written permission of the publisher except in the case of brief quotations embodied in critical articles and reviews.

ISBN: 978-1-4525-0327-1 (sc)
978-1-4525-0328-8 (e)

Balboa Press books may be ordered through booksellers or by contacting:

Balboa Press
A Division of Hay House
1663 Liberty Drive
Bloomington, IN 47403
www.balboapress.com
1-(877) 407-4847

Because of the dynamic nature of the Internet, any web addresses or links contained in this book may have changed since publication and may no longer be valid. The views expressed in this work are solely those of the author and do not necessarily reflect the views of the publisher, and the publisher hereby disclaims any responsibility for them.

Any people depicted in stock imagery provided by Thinkstock are models, and such images are being used for illustrative purposes only. Certain stock imagery © Thinkstock.

Printed in the United States of America

Balboa Press rev. date: 05/16/2012

Preface

"There is so much more to life than meets the everyday eye, so much more than we are led to believe. We are not here by some coincidence of nature. Our lives are precious, with deep meaning and profound purpose. Valarie Coventry's new book expertly explains this process. We have lived countless times in many different bodies, as our soul progresses along its spiritual path.

Filled with fascinating stories from her clients, "Your Soul Is Calling You" documents the many types of healing that past life regression therapy can accomplish. Beyond physical and emotional healing and beyond the repair of broken relationships lie the incredible vistas of spiritual understanding and enlightened perspective. Reading this book, which is a pleasant and uplifting experience, can lead to a deep and positive transformation in your values and your life.

For the past twenty years my wife, Carole, and I have taught techniques of past life regression therapy to therapists from all over the world. To document past life memories and the powerful healing effects that accompany such recall is one of our most important goals. It's very gratifying to have our student and colleague, Valarie, continue this work in Australia and write such a delightful book."

Brian L. Weiss, M.D.
Author of "Many Lives, Many Masters"

'The Cheesewring' - Herts, UK

SOUL CALLS

Acknowledgements

I owe a debt of gratitude to Brian and Carole Weiss for their wonderful professional workshop and their help in guiding my first clumsy footsteps in the amazing field of regression work. Doubtless, I will have the opportunity to repay this debt in our next incarnation together, I look forward to that.

Also in gratitude for my soul family that chose to incarnate with me; my wonderful sons Leigh and Simon and my amazing daughter in law Dana, thank you for choosing me this time around; I look forward to more lifetimes with you. As for my beautiful grand daughters Zaya and Lani, I am so thankful to be such an instrumental part of their young lives and I look forward to being a part of the passing on of knowledge to the next generation of healers to come. The world needs them.

For my parents - gratitude comes with understanding why it had to be so hard.

Heartfelt thanks for the love and support of Geoff and Glenys; the karmic lessons that I have learned from both of you have deepened my understanding of myself and strengthened my spiritual belief and I thank you for the gifts that have come from that.

To all my wonderful women friends, in particular Annie with whom I travelled to the UK to take my first tentative steps into rediscovering my spiritual heritage, and Leonie who generously gave of her time and ideas and editing support. Thank you my friends-you know who you are.

For those wonderful women in my women's circle who are coming into their power now, Emma, Lynn, Gill, Sheryl and Sandy and past circle members-I am so pleased to have been a part of your journey. Also, Michelle, Claire, Deb, Judy, Jenny, Pat, Nan and others now in spirit, thank you for your continuing guidance.

For technical assistance, grateful thanks to Kate Gryguc of Global Graphics for rose image and CD covers, Gerhard for photographing my artwork so beautifully and Willard and Jenna from Balboa Press for their patient assistance. Also Leon Nacson of Hay House for his initial encouragement.

Finally, and most importantly, a big thank you to those clients who gave me permission to share their stories so that others could benefit from their experience. Without you, this book would not have been written-you are truly inspirational!

Contents

Preface *1*
Acknowledgements *4*
Introduction *6*

SECTION 1 JOURNEY OF THE SOUL 9
CHAPTER 1 My regression story 11
CHAPTER 2 The Regression experience 13

SECTION 2 KARMIC RELATIONSHIPS 19
CHAPTER 3 Rachel's story 21
CHAPTER 4 Mark and James' story 25
CHAPTER 5 Annabelle's story 31
CHAPTER 6 Pauline's story 35
CHAPTER 7 David's story 37

SECTION 3 EMOTIONAL HEALING 41
CHAPTER 8 Bonnie's story 43
CHAPTER 9 Janie's story 45
CHAPTER 10 Linda's story 49
CHAPTER 11 Nina's story 51

SECTION 4 HEALING TRAUMA AND PHOBIAS 57
CHAPTER 12 Donna's story 59
CHAPTER 13 Fiona's story 63
CHAPTER 14 Mandy's story 65

SECTION 5 PHYSICAL HEALING 69
CHAPTER 15 Mary's story 71
CHAPTER 16 Gloria's story 75
CHAPTER 17 Cheri's story 77
CHAPTER 18 Annie's story 81

SECTION 6 SPIRITUAL DEVELOPMENT 85
CHAPTER 19 Jilly's story 87
CHAPTER 20 Ruth's story 89
CHAPTER 21 Andrew's story 93
CHAPTER 22 Sarah's story 97
CHAPTER 23 Bluebirds 100

Summary *102*
Author profile *105*
Recommended reading *109*

Introduction

A call from the soul generally comes in one of two ways. For some, it is a knowing which grows into a deep conviction that leads to action. For others, it feels more like a whap on the head or being shaken until your teeth rattle which serves, literally, as a wake up call. Let me give you an example of the first; the second comes later in my story.

In 1997 following my emigration from the UK in 1973, I realized that I had spent an equal amount of time in both Australia and the UK without feeling really connected at a soul level to either one. I had no real sense of belonging to either country. My birth family were all in the UK, my husband and my two sons were Australian and here I was, sort of floating somewhere in the middle. Around this time, I became caught up in the wave of New Age spiritual awareness which was capturing the imagination and hearts of so many others around me. It was as if we couldn't get enough of indigenous spirituality. My husband and I decided to attend a "Spirit of the Earth" conference in Kalgoorlie in which Elders from many different cultures were coming together to share their knowledge in an attempt to raise awareness of the need to respect the Earth and all its inhabitants.

As we awaited the first speaker, a Native American Indian named Lightening Bear, I glanced around at the audience. Everywhere I looked there were westerners like me wearing colourful dress, Indian jewellery and some with eagle feathers tucked into their hatbands. A hush came over the audience as Lightening Bear took the podium. What an arresting figure! Over six foot tall, in traditional Native American Indian dress and with long braids flanking his angular body, he quietly surveyed the audience for several minutes. You could sense that there wasn't one tiny detail that those deep set hooded eyes missed. People began to cough nervously and shuffle their feet as his gaze fell upon them, it was a brave person who met those eyes head on. Quietly he began to speak, of the plight of Mother Earth, the lack of respect for the land and her indigenous peoples and the urgent need for us to share in the custodianship of the earth for Her to survive. We could no longer just take what we wanted, he said, and expect the Earth to go on giving. It was time to give something back and we were all on notice. Again his gaze rested on the audience thoughtfully.
"I see some of you wear eagle feathers in your hats. In our culture, eagle feather have to be earned and are a mark of the great respect given to that person." He waited. Some people furtively removed their adorned hats and looked at the ground, perhaps in embarrassment or shame.
"You must look amongst your own stories for your answers," he said gently.
His message was simple yet given in a loving manner. "We cannot help you with your search for your own spirituality, but we will respect your customs and your ways and we are willing to share our knowledge and work together to ensure the survival of our Mother Earth." He was followed by another respected Elder from the Amazon rainforests who spoke of the white man's desecration of their forests for monetary gain. Again, what struck me was the lack of censure in his voice as he asked for us to heed the message before it was too late.

My soul call came directly from this experience as a deep yearning for information and stories about my own Celtic background which would not go away no matter how busy I kept myself. My only experience of religion was of fainting through the torment of the Sunday service as a child. Each week, one of the clergy would sit behind me with a glass of water at the ready for the moment when the stars would begin to swirl before my eyes, and each week without fail, I would wake up lying on the hard wooden bench outside the church feeling nauseated and about as far from God as you could get. The only mystery as far as I was concerned, was why my parents continued to send me knowing that this would happen. It was time for me to go back to the land of the Celts and discover my spiritual heritage.

This turned out to be a real adventure as I travelled the ley lines across England, scientist friend in tow, following the footsteps of my ancestors from one sacred site to another. From this experience, the seeds of the idea for this book were sown. However, had I known how completely this journey would change my life, I'm not sure that I would have had the courage to keep going.

The second soul call came on my return to Australia. Coming from the relative peace of the sacred areas in which I had been travelling, I found the noise and busyness of what I had previously thought of as "normal" life overwhelming. Within weeks, I had moved down south to the peaceful rural area of Western Australia where I picked up one of Brian Weiss's books, 'Many Lives, Many Masters' to read. Mesmerised by his stories of the deep healing that his clients had experienced through regression work, I turned to the end of the book. The address in America almost leapt out at me from the page, and in a moment of déjà vu, I knew, without any shadow of a doubt, that I would be training with him and furthering his regression work in Australia. That was my second soul call.

The Journey

SECTION I

JOURNEY OF THE SOUL

CHAPTER 1
My regression story

It was no small feat to pack up, leave a family and venture off to the other side of the world on my own, but soul calls cannot be ignored. I can still remember the amazement of some of the other participants at his professional training in Rhinebeck, New York. "You've come from Australia?" they queried, in disbelief. Although there were over a hundred professionals there from all parts of the world, I had travelled the furthest!
During this training, I was to experience a most powerful healing that took me completely by surprise; but first, the magic of being there with Brian and Carole at the first workshop.

Brian was the most gentle, unassuming man I had ever come across, which made his stage regressions with selected audience members even more powerful. How I longed to be one of them, but with so many of us eager to volunteer, he was only able to do a limited number of demonstrations before encouraging us to practice in small groups. Visualise over one hundred people in a hall filled to capacity, with small group regressions going on everywhere, and you can imagine the noise level! I was feeling disappointed at not having experienced a personal regression with Brian, and when it was my turn to be 'regressed' in my group, I clearly remember thinking as I laid down on the hard floor, "Yeah, like this is really going to work with all this racket going on!" I was acutely aware of all the background noise as one of the American women in my group led me through the induction process.

My mind was wandering to different parts of the hall, hearing snatches of conversation here and there, when suddenly I felt my body jolting and my head 'turned' to look over my right side. (In fact, I was to find out later that I had not moved my body at all at that point). In some amazement, I found myself 'looking down' at the wooden wheel of a cart as it was jolting along a cobbled street. At the same time as my subconscious mind was registering this, I was clearly aware of my conscious mind thinking "aahh, that's why it's jolting, because its carved out of one solid piece of wood and they couldn't get it perfectly round in those days." It was the most bizarre experience to be experiencing something on one level and understanding it on another, and yet, in that moment, it felt like the most natural thing in the world. Shortly after, I became aware of an uncomfortable feeling of restriction in my legs, as if they were bound or tied in some way. Afterwards, the women told me that I was rubbing my two legs up and down against each other, as though I was trying to free them. Although I was unaware of this at the time, it was only later that I made the connection between this experience and the physical symptoms that I was experiencing in this lifetime.

Apparently, it was at the time of the Inquisition and I was being taken on a wooden cart to be burned at the stake as a witch, simply for practicing my healing arts. Strangely enough, I wasn't scared, just angry. How dare they punish me (and many others like me) just for trying to help people who needed healing! I was frustrated by their stupidity rather than the act of violence itself, and was very aware that it was directed at men, specifically those connected with the Church. I have a vague recollection of flames and lots of jeering faces, although, ten years later, the details are not as clear, even though the experience itself is as vivid now as it was then. Strangely, I felt no pain during this death scene although I was acutely aware of my thoughts and feelings of betrayal.

The whole experience seemed to last a few minutes, although afterwards I found out that my regression had taken almost an hour. Later, I discovered that time distortion is a common element of regression work and indeed, in the many regressions I have done since, most people are amazed at how long they have been 'under.' The restriction in my legs was indeed because they were bound with rope, but what was even more amazing to me was that I had suffered very badly from psoriasis for the last twenty years, particularly on my legs at the exact place where I had felt the ropes rubbing! In fact, I was so embarrassed about it that I always wore long pants rather than skirts or dresses because it looked so unsightly. The disease had manifested during the time of my divorce from my first husband who had left me just before the birth of our son. The theme of betrayal from this past life had been repeated in my current life! There was obviously a lesson here for me to learn.

After the regression, my facilitator, a wonderful American woman called Carol, who was also there as a participant, told me that she felt intuitively that my anger was linked with the unsightly rash on my legs. She told me that it was the first layer of healing but she encouraged me to keep working on this issue so that they could heal completely. Thankfully, someone had the presence of mind to suggest taking a photograph of my legs, badly scarred with the psoriasis, for future 'proof'. The healing process started after the regression and continued until they had almost completely cleared about six months later. Now, whenever I get that itchy feeling, it is a cue to look at where I feel angry or constricted in my life and serves as a timely reminder to let go of any judgement or negative emotions surrounding my experience. My own regression story, taken from that time in America, demonstrated to me the healing that can come from such experiences.

On my return, I began to use regression work with clients, tentatively at first, then with increasing confidence as the results spoke for themselves. The theory that our experiences are held within our cellular memories makes perfect sense when I reflect upon the emotional and physical healing that I, and many of my clients, experience during regression work. Once the memory is released and made conscious, the healing seems to automatically follow in most cases. I have even had a case of spontaneous healing from a client with long term pain in the breast despite the fact that the woman I was regressing doubted that her experience was real. She later wrote to me to tell me that, to this day, her symptom has never returned. Her story appears later in the book.

I will forever be grateful to Brian for his influence on my work. I am sure that we have shared a lifetime together and when I looked into his twinkling eyes during his visit to Australia some ten years later, I could sense that he too remembered.

CHAPTER 2
The Regression experience

"Really important meetings are planned by the soul long before the bodies see each other. Generally speaking, these meetings occur when we reach a limit, when we need to die and be reborn emotionally. These meetings are waiting for us, but more often that not, we avoid them happening. If we are desperate, though, if we have nothing to lose, or if we are full of enthusiasm for life, then the unknown reveals itself, and our universe changes direction.
Everyone knows how to love, because we are all born with that gift. Some people have a natural talent for it, but the majority of us have to re-learn, to remember how to love, and everyone, without exception, needs to burn on the bonfire of past emotions, to re-live certain joys and griefs, certain ups and downs, until they can see the connecting thread that exists behind each new encounter; because there is a connecting thread." Paulo Coelho "Eleven Minutes" Harper Collins 2003

The focus of my work is to help individuals gain insight on the spiritual lessons they are here to learn. The regression experience offers an opportunity to experience that connecting thread, and, by understanding the lessons attached to those learning experiences, to clear the emotional pain attached to past events. Being part of a regression experience is like watching a story unfold. The process of tracking back through childhood experiences, birth memories and past lives almost always reveals common threads; themes such as betrayal, misuse of power, lost love seem to come up repeatedly until the lessons are understood and the emotional pain that is attached to them can be released from cellular memory.

Much has already been written about cellular memory but it was only relatively recently, according to Roger Woolger* that research validated the notion of internalisation of our life scripts from birth as part of our psychic make up. In his excellent book 'Other Lives, Other Selves', he details several case histories of clients unconsciously living out their parent's scripts, particularly those of the mother with whom they were more intimately connected in the womb. My own experiences of cellular memory release demonstrated to me the impact of other energetic influences on the physical body. Many years ago when I first began working in the healing field, I offered massage as a treatment modality. I clearly remember one woman who burst into sobs when I began to gently massage her hands. My touch had triggered a vivid memory of being held down by her hands while she was being raped, and although her unconscious had previously blocked the memory to protect her, the healing that came from the release of that cellular memory was deep and lasting.

Another of my clients reported a conversation that he had over heard while in utero which was later able to be confirmed by his astonished parents who had been discussing the pros and cons of an abortion. His parents were adamant that they had never discussed their ambivalence around the pregnancy with him.[1]
Some years after my own regression experience, I was fortunate enough to receive some energetic healing from a woman whose matriarchal line was devoted to this ancient and sacred practice. She worked mainly on my belly and legs where she 'felt' much emotion was buried. The healing went deeper than I could have imagined, and, several days later, I was covered in red, itchy spots over those very areas of my body. As I felt the old, buried emotional pain just

---
[1] *R Woolger:Other Lives, Other Selves (1988)-A Jungian Psychotherapist Discovers past Lives.

dissolve away during the sessions, my body continued to fight to release the physical effects of those experiences which had been trapped in my body for so many years.

For a whole month, as I struggled with the desire to scratch and tear at my skin, the words "I have to get out," repeated over and over in my head, triggering an adolescent memory of hiding in my bedroom with my hands over my ears while my parents were arguing, usually about me. I could literally feel the heat surging from one place to another in my body seeking release as the spots kept popping up, first in one part of my body then moving to another, as I once again experienced the anger of feeling trapped in a situation which was outside of my control. It was a very similar to the emotions I experienced during my regression to the time of the Inquisition. After a month, the rest of the psoriasis had completely disappeared along with the spots and for the first time in my life, I felt completely free of the influence of my restrictive childhood on an emotional level

"We must enjoy this life now," Pilar told me during my final session, "and when it is time to go back, we just go back." She shrugged her shoulders; to her it was just as simple as that. Her wise words remain with me and offer a healing perspective on the loss of those we love. We none of us know how long we have and to assume that we are all meant to live to a 'ripe old age' makes loss much more difficult to deal with. For some, our time here on earth is a much shorter time than others, but how much more important it then becomes to really value each other and really live each day of your life - no matter what it brings.

The regression experience offers a much broader perspective on life. To witness the repeating pattern of our experiences as we struggle with our lessons, offers a context in which to understand our spiritual contract and identify the lessons that we are here to learn.

It is not 'who you were' in a past life that is important, or even what happened, but what you learned about yourself from those experiences. The lessons that were behind them and how they relate to your current life are the blueprint for your soul's purpose. A good facilitator is able to help you uncover those experiences without leading you with questions or interpreting events for you. Skilful and appropriate questioning together with compassion for the client are the most important qualities that a regression therapist can have, as any question that is posed has the potential to take the client off track into the therapist's mindset. The only questions that are truly helpful are those which encourage clients to describe their experience. All we need to do as facilitators is to pace the session accordingly to assist the individual to meet their stated goals.

Often the most powerful processing is at work during periods of silence, while the person makes sense of their experience in their own minds, and they always do. It is not for us to decide what they are here to learn.

It has also been very valuable for me to witness that everyone processes information differently. Sometimes the clues are in the person's language – another reason why the intake of information prior to a regression is so important. Some people do indeed 'see' whole movies, but, in my experience, these are relatively rare. The majority of individuals have fragments or images that come to them in pieces. The more they can trust the validity of those images, the more they develop into a meaningful story. Others, whose dominant sensory mode is feeling, will most likely feel their experiences rather than see them and a small percentage of individuals will hear conversations, maybe in conjunction with some imagery, some not.

One of the most memorable regressions I conducted was for a woman who was unable to see anything, but who felt unable to move for most of the session. She had come to see me with issues around intimacy and complained of feeling 'stuck,' unable to get what she wanted from life. However, towards the end of the session, as we explored the purple haze that was all that she could distinguish, a wooden post seemed to develop in the periphery of her mind which she

found very puzzling, until she finally identified it as the post at the end of her crib. Currently trapped in a loveless marriage and with no means of financial support, she was reliving this first memory of feeling powerless as a baby.
"I am lying on my side with my neck at an odd angle," she told me. "I want to look to the left shoulder but my neck feels stuck…am pressed up against something. My face and shoulder are against something…my head is pushed down to the left and sort of looking behind (at this point she was lying perfectly straight on the mattress in my office) I am trying to move my head to look up but can't see anything. There is pressure in the left side of my neck; it is at an angle to my shoulder. I am looking back and up, my left leg is stiff and heavy. I am stuck in a corner and can't move…I am stuck. I am little and chubby and I want someone to come and get me, I want to get out, but no one comes and I am just stuck there. It is dark where I am but there is light to the right. Don't understand why I can't move."

The regressions that she experienced allowed her to see that this theme of being trapped had repeated itself throughout her whole life and motivated her to take control and make some important changes. I have found that the memories often come up in a backward sequence. It is therefore not unusual for current life memories to come first before past life experiences and neither do I suggest that a client goes to a past life unless they have expressly asked for that experience. It is my experience that the subconscious mind, which is the repository for all memories, knows where to go and in what sequence. It is a matter of trusting your own intuition and 'going with it' rather than analysing or questioning the experience.

When clients ask if their memories are real or imagined, I tell them that there is no way of knowing for sure. However, there are many instances of details from the past being verified, notably by Dr Ian Stevenson of the University of Virginia. Dr Stevenson's attempts to prove the reincarnation experience involved exhaustive research into past life experiences from various countries, notably India where reincarnation is an accepted teaching. More importantly, these regression experiences have the power to heal; so whether they are metaphors, actual memories or a creation of the mind becomes less important than how a person's life can change for the better from the experience. The guilt goes, the mind is more peaceful and the spirit understands the lesson(s). It is often the case that the spiritual aspects of a person's life become more important after experiencing a regression. In this aspect, there is a similarity to near death experiences where the individual is able to witness events from a higher perspective which leads to a greater understanding of our life on earth. Some good references have been included in the appendices for those interested in exploring this topic further.

However, interesting confirmations do occur in regressions which support the idea that they are much more complex than the imagination alone can produce. Apart from the strong emotions that usually accompany such experiences, the historical synchronicities can be quite compelling. Annie's regression was such a case.
She had come complaining of long term problems with her throat which had not responded to any kind of treatment. Her symptoms were so severe, that she was unable to rest her head in alignment with her body while lying down; instead she had to tuck her jaw into her chest as if to protect her throat. During her regression she began to gag as though she was choking;
"Pressure on my throat and neck," she gasped, "water rising up inside me…heaviness on my chest, can't breathe, darkness…think I am buried! Feel it in my leg now, my left side is raised up somehow." Then, later;
"I see a little town, built on a hill. Tall thin white buildings-orange tiled roofs. There's been a landslide. See old lady, grandma figure, grey shawl, long grey black skirt, white lacy bonnet. Beam of wood, feel like it is connected to uncomfortable sensation in leg, going through my body on an angle." She also saw a man frantically digging in the mud, trying to find her. "He will never give up," she says, "even though he will never find me." Some time after the regression, she wrote to me.

I thought you might be interested in hearing what I have been researching after my last regression. I don't know if you remember this; after you had guided me out of the regression, I mentioned Tuscany, at the time I thought it was in France. I googled houses in Tuscany and discovered little villages built on the hillsides, just like the one I saw. The thing that confirmed my regression experience for me, was the realisation that a lot of those villages did, and still do, suffer from landslides! The one I was drawn to was Sorano which experienced a devastating landslide in 1801. However, last night I discovered a village called Savignon which is north of Tuscany. It has an uncanny resemblance to the one in my regression."

Annie's symptoms were greatly relieved after her regression. You can find the fascinating story behind the healing of the uncomfortable itching in her navel later in the book in the section on Physical Healings. Perhaps more importantly for her, it helped to heal her relationship with her father who was the one frantically trying to dig her out of the mudslide. Over protective in the extreme in her current life, he was no doubt living with the unconscious fear that something would happen that he could not save her from. Understanding this enabled her to be more compassionate towards him.

In the stories which follow, names and other identifying information have been changed to protect the privacy of individuals. However, their actual stories are reproduced as they unfolded during the regressions. Where there is significant interaction in a session, italics have been used to distinguish the therapist's comments. Elsewhere, they have been used to reference direct quotations or client feedback from follow up letters.

PERSONAL NOTES

Dance of the Earth Goddess

SECTION 2

KARMIC RELATIONSHIPS

CHAPTER 3
Rachel's story

Much has been written about soul mates and the notion of there being one perfect soul mate for everyone. Understandably, this can set up unrealistic expectations in intimate relationships and lead to anxiety that one might have somehow failed to connect with the one person that could bring happiness in this lifetime.
Both Brian Weiss and Roger Woolger refer to the notion of soul groups and functioning as a family of souls in which we choose to reincarnate again with specific individuals with whom we are emotionally connected. They suggest that their bodies and the nature of our relationships with them may change across lifetimes as we choose to experience differing forms of intimacy together.

I have noticed that frustration can develop in relationships when one party feels that they are progressing more quickly along their spiritual path, seemingly learning and growing from their life experiences while they perceive that their partner seems content to coast along. Yet we cannot be responsible for another person's spiritual development – that is their choice. They may choose not to embrace the concept at all in this life and all we can do is to hold them in a place of love and compassion and focus on our own journey. Ultimately, this may mean letting go of the relationship if it becomes detrimental to our own growth, although it is always worth remembering that if we do not make a conscious effort to deal with the issues that arise in our relationships, we are destined to repeat the same pattern over and over again in the future until we understand the lesson being presented. The most important lessons are often mirrored by our conflicts with our partners and families and it takes courage and patience to deal with them honestly and objectively.

This having been said, I am sure we all know couples who fit the description of 'Twin Souls.' They operate as two halves of one whole and their lives are devoted to each other to the exclusion of all others. Often married for many years, they find themselves unable to live without the other and usually follow them very quickly to the Afterlife. On the other end of the continuum, the most challenging and difficult relationships are offering us the opportunity to develop those very qualities that we are lacking in ourselves. The very nature of karmic relationships seems to draw us to those individuals who reflect opposite qualities to the ones that we possess; we are attracted by their very difference. The cosmic joke is that we then often tend to expend a lot of energy trying to convince them to be more like us! There is much to be gained by taking a step back during times of conflict, taking a broader view and asking ourselves, what am I meant to learn from this situation?
The following stories all identify different aspects of soul mate relationships and serve to shed light on the reasons that the individuals came together.

Rachel was a lovely young woman who had come to me through unfortunate circumstances. Her fiancé had died unexpectedly at a young age and she was overwhelmed with grief. He had been her 'soul mate.' Her family were very worried about her and she seemed unable to move on with her life without him by her side.

We worked together for quite some time before we attempted a regression. This was necessary, for her own healing, to work through her grief as a priority. Nevertheless, she found the concept of reincarnation a very comforting one. During the course of her counselling, I had lent her one of Brian Weiss's books. She found it fascinating and was eager for more information and I lent her more books on the topic. As she began to heal, we began to talk more and more about past lives. We did several regressions together; her first experiences remain private-she was able to reconnect with her lost love and that brought her much comfort. This one was some time later, when she was moving forward but still 'going through the motions' rather than getting any enjoyment out of her life. She tended to push herself very hard in an effort to create a sense of independence but felt that an essential ingredient was missing. It was at this point that I felt a regression might help.

Rachel was very comfortable with me and able to enter a trance state very quickly, as evidenced by the rapid movement of her eyes under their lids.

"Gold ring on hand, darker skin," she recounted quickly; "dark red dress…I'm somewhere…all made of wood, like a pub…really old, other people around…olden days kind of clothes. Man behind bar pouring beer…wearing little gold earrings." Just as quickly as she was able to tell me what was happening, the scene changed again.

"Cemetery…crying…ages ago," she informed me, "grass really green, headstone really white. My hair's really nice," she remembers smiling. "I look lovely…have red lipstick on…young…in my 20's or 30's. Can see a statue of older lady – an angel!" she exclaims. "Big wings…black wrought iron fence…don't think I'm supposed to love the person I'm crying for. Can see the headstone - Henry 1944." I am amazed at the detail in which she is viewing this and wait for her to continue. There is no need for questions; I am merely a witness to what appears like a very vivid past life.

"I was rich and he was poor," she explains to me. "We loved each other. I'm really depressed, I don't like my life…I have money." Her ability to switch between present and past tense is an indication of the shift that occurs between the unconscious mind which recounts the 'memory' and the conscious mind which is able to explain and analyse at the same time. It is fascinating to observe.

After a pause during which her eyelids flicker rapidly as she continues to process the images, she continues. "There's a man, he's angry with me…brown suit, little hat. Brother…little brother…he's telling me not to be upset." I ask her what stands out the most for her.

"The colours of everything; my skin's really white…really pretty…black hair. That person understood me."

"What happened to him?" I ask.

"He was killed," she says sadly, "shot purposefully…to do with me. My dress is silk, satin."

It seems there is a difference in class-they weren't allowed to be together and he paid the price for their relationship.

"What is important for you to know from this?" I ask her, wondering about the lesson to be learned.

"Someone else might understand me, doesn't have to be my family. Having lots of possessions doesn't make you happy…can be miserable with them. I had so much fun with this person. He was younger than me…brunette hair, made me laugh and enjoy life heaps. Selfish…I'm going to be by myself. It's hard to do, be by myself," she adds and I note the chords that resonate through both lives and the difficulties of coping alone after the loss of her love.

"Don't think I knew that person well," she observes finally. "I look like I have given up. My family have really had enough of me. I didn't realise that I didn't have it beforehand. This person has taught me about life, to have fun, enjoy it and laugh, relax. Things that we think matter, don't matter," she explains.

"What do you tell yourself about his death?" I ask her, wondering if there is a link with the death of her fiancé in this life.

"I'm going to change my ways," she tells me confidently, "live how he lived. Even though it was a friendship, we loved each other. Value what's important. Even though I'm supposed to do certain things (by my family) I'm a really strong personality, determined. Find this place where strength resides – that real core…tenacity…must be there."

"This quality is not lost," I reassure her, "you can have it now-find the place in your body where it resides."

"Old and alone…" She ignores me, still very much in her story. "She clung on to what she had. She had really good hair-even at the end…grey hair, all neatly done…was ready to die." I ask what her last thoughts were.

"Couldn't wait to see that guy again…loved her family. Even though that happened, she didn't want anything else to happen for them." I presume she is talking about not taking the friendship further because of the repercussions and wonder aloud about the lesson(s) behind the experience.

"Her steely determination got in the way of something. She didn't let go, so couldn't let any new love in. She always felt alone, loved her brother. Although determination is good, if it gets in the way of letting new things in, it is counter productive. I can enjoy myself and still use my determination for something else," she realises.

I am happy for her that she has identified the lesson, knowing that it is much more important for her to understand the learning experience than for me to know what it is about.

Rachel seemed more at peace with herself after this regression and did indeed appear to be more open to having fun and enjoying some new experiences. I was very happy for her; the death of her fiancé at such an early age had been a cruel blow. She had grieved for a long time and this represented a step forward. Later, she wondered aloud whether he had contracted with her before this life to leave early so that she could develop her independence and pursue her spiritual growth. It offered her some comfort to think that they would meet again in a future life.

CHAPTER 4
Mark and James' story

Mark came for a regression to establish if he had experienced a past life with his current partner and as a part of his own spiritual journey to which he was deeply committed. A friendly and charming young man, I could immediately see how well suited he was to his role in marketing. He was enthusiastic about the prospect of a regression and life in general.

After the usual induction, he began to breathe very deeply and I asked him to choose a childhood memory and to describe it as it was happening. He responded very quickly. "I'm under a table…outdoor table…blue tarpaulin over it, I'm underneath it, hiding…colour blue. Very young, I'm naked, it's sunny, I'm hiding from Mum." There was nothing more, and as he did not seem to be overly perturbed, I asked him to go to an earlier childhood memory that seemed important.
"Can see Mum…she's in a hospital bed. Can't describe myself. Think Dad's there too…just seem to be watching, don't think I am there. She's sad and confused."
"Why is she there?" I ask, wondering if he is remembering his own birth.
"A baby…just after," he confirms.
(Often this can happen, that a person regresses to the time of their birth or in utero and does not have a sense of their own body, only that they know what is happening for the mother at the time of the birth)
He gives signals that he is anxious to move on and I direct him, as he had requested, to a past life.
"I'm in a field," he tells me, "might be wheat…big field. There's a tractor…red tractor…someone on a tractor…blue overalls…house in the distance. Tractor's going towards the house. He's old, beard…white… old tractor. House is white, two storeys, like you see in the movies. Doesn't seem to be anyone else in the house. It's dusty, old; somewhere in America…he grows wheat. Flat, sunny, 1940's. Feel there's no one else there, just man on the tractor. He has to get on with it, just keep doing what he's doing."
"Is he happy?' I ask curiously.
"He doesn't know, he just keeps going. He's on the front porch of his house, very sad, everything has aged around him…he's just stayed there, looking out. He's very alone…sad." There seems to be no further elaboration.
"Go to the time directly after this life, after he has passed," I direct him. There is silence for a while and then his head moves to one side as though he is listening.
"I'm in white, there's someone there…he's a monk…seems familiar." He frowns as though he is concentrating.
"Look into his eyes," I encourage him, wondering if this could be the connection he is searching for.
"He's trying to get me to remember…feel him smile. I feel like I didn't pay attention, closed off. Need to be aware, be open…didn't do any of it." He sounds despondent.
"What is the contract for your next incarnation?"
"Do what I'm meant to do, be open and learn, realize who I am."
"Do you understand this now?" I ask.
"Yes…not be close minded, and trust."
"Go to your life review"
"Others are there. I can't tell who they are."

"Go to another life that's important for you." I trust that his unconscious will know where to go.

"Feels like an old street, people everywhere, long time ago…carriages and horses…ladies…grey, people going about their business. I'm in the street…have shoes on…big buckles. Want to drink beer!" He chuckles.

"Where are you?"

"I'm outside a tavern…go in…it's noisy. I shouldn't be there, I look out of place, but it's ok, they know me. They're commoners, I'm not, but it's ok. I am Richard-I drink beer!" He laughs heartily. "I've got more money. They like me; I look like the rest of them."

"You sound happy in this life," I remark.

"I mix with them, they're more real. I buy them beer!" He laughs again, amused by this.

"Is there anyone there you recognize?"

"Yes, there's someone…he's at the bar…we always talk. He's a commoner, that's ok. He always says he would buy me beer but he doesn't have the money, but it's ok…I buy it for him." He doesn't seem to recognize the person and I encourage him to move on.

"Can you move forward in this life?"

"Other rich people like me. Someone kills me, stabs me in the chest. I know him!"

"Who is this person?"

"Rival," he says shortly. "He's jealous because I'm happy. I mix with others and not with him, not his kind…I bring shame on all the rest by mixing with these commoners."

"Who is there at your death, at your grave?"

"Commoners, they've come from everywhere!" He sounds surprised.

"They liked you." I affirm it for him.

"I'm sad to leave, will miss them."

"Go to the time after this lifetime. What are the lessons to be learned?"

"Share…be brave and go out on your own. I achieved that. Don't know if I should have got them all drunk though!" He chuckles again, then adds "it's what I feel, learn to love, but there's no one there," he says sadly.

"Go to a previous life time with your current partner."

"I'm swimming. I'm only a little boy…another boy there too…having fun…best friends. He's skinny, black hair, playful and joyful…Jack."

"You have fun together," I observe.

"All the time…he's gone now!" There is real anguish in his voice.

"What happened to him?"

"Don't know…it hurts… we were always together…he's left." He is heartbroken. It seems that the family moved away. I leave him with the emotion for a while, knowing that re-experiencing it will help heal him.

"Do you see him again?"

"I sense him, I feel him. Can't move, can't breathe. I feel something's missing. We used to live next door to each other - he just left – the house was just empty!"

"What do you tell yourself about this experience?"

"We have been together before and will do again. It's like a joke," he laughs. "Jack forgets and wonders why. Not this time, he's James."

"What are the lessons from this life?"

"Remember; gently, gently guide each other…so we remember. Be open." There is silence for a while as he processes this, then he adds, "still a lesson to learn about loss. I teach him the same lesson he taught me. I have to go away-he will have to learn but we will laugh about it later. I have to make him comfortable with that. I'm trying, I'm trying. He's going to…" his next words are indecipherable.

"You can help him understand this, that this is not the end," I suggest.

"Yes, I need to do it sooner…surrounded by death. Need to make sure he is ok, will be ok. All part of the growing – trying to remember is the hardest part. Intensity, study the afterlife. Living a spiritual life with full knowledge…live with the big picture in mind. I will die before him." He is objective about this.

"Do you want to come back now?"

"Yes." He leaves content, having found his past love and knowing that he is on his spiritual path.

Some weeks later, when I followed him up, he had this to say about the impact of the regression on his life.

The biggest thing for me was trust, trusting the regression process and letting it unfold and trusting the information that came through. How would I know it's real and not just a figment of my imagination? It was the emotion behind it that gave me an indication there was something else going on here that I wasn't consciously in control of. Deep emotion linked to the events I was describing welled up causing tears to flow and I realised no matter how creative my imagination was, I could never have created such powerful emotions.

The information I got out of the regression cemented what I already 'sort of' felt' about my relationships and life purpose, but now only deepened them. Some sort of new creative power was unleashed as only a month afterward I started doing some drawings with a spiritual twist which has now resulted in a multi book deal with a publisher. My life purpose was to show people how to live with the big picture in mind and enjoy a spiritual life and I feel I'm now doing that.

Once again, I felt humbled by the feedback and tremendously grateful to Brian Weiss for assisting me to do this kind of work. To my great delight, Mark's partner James contacted me two months later for a regression. Much taken by Mark's story and the effect that the regression had made to his life, he was now ready to explore his own soul's purpose and, hopefully, clear any issues that were standing in the way of his progress.

Shy and reserved in manner, James was nervous when he arrived and we spent some time talking to enable him to feel comfortable. I asked him how they had met and noted how his eyes lit up when he spoke of his partner. There was an unmistakeable attraction when they met, he told me. Both had been in other relationships when they were first introduced and, from that moment, they knew that they belonged together. This is typical of karmic relationships, that immediate spark of recognition speaks of a connection that goes back to other lifetimes together. As partners in a gay relationship, James had developed a protective shell around himself. Remaining private was his defence against criticism and judgement, however, underneath the shell, he constantly criticised himself and hid his vulnerability. Only his partner knew the extent of his deep sadness and even his love was not enough to keep the demons away.

I took extra time to relax James as much as possible before regressing him to a childhood memory. To my relief, he was able to access a clear memory almost immediately.

"Farmhouse…outside. Just got back from somewhere," he told me. "It's raining lots…windy. I'm very young, thin, and little, about five. Just got out of the car…front veranda…parcel on top, in brown paper and string – it's for me," he exclaims in pleasure. He realises that it is a birthday present for him and opens it in excitement which quickly turns to disappointment.

"Red jumper, grandmother has knitted it…it's really, really big…don't think I will ever wear it," he says sadly.

"What stands out the most for you from this memory?"

"Rain…weather…really red colour, softness of the wool," he replies. I ask him to go back further to an earlier memory as an infant or a toddler, trying to get a sense of how he felt growing up as a child.

"I'm a baby, in a cane bassinet…white…in the back seat of a car. I'm the only one, mum and dad are in the front seat… there's lines in the sky…like tram lines," he explains. "They criss cross, can see them through the back window… smell the leather of the seats." I ask him if he is aware of how he feels, wondering about the significance of this clear memory.

"I'm OK," he says, "I'm aware of my parents just driving…just interested in the lines." There is nothing further and as he seems to be quite comfortable in his ability to recall, I decide to instruct his subconscious to take him back to the source of his current problems.

"I'm in darkness," he says immediately, "deep sadness…old man…big white beard, no hair on his head. Just sitting in a hut…only one room…he just sits there. Dark outside…he doesn't have anyone there…he's alone…he doesn't know what to do…just resting on one elbow…staring straight ahead. Everyone has left him." He is hardly breathing, as though he has given up, and I question him gently.

"How is it for him?'

"He's not very nice…this is why he was left," he informs me, sounding sad. "Now he has no one…very alone…he knows they won't come back."

"Go forward to the end of his life, what happens to him?"

"He dies in the hut…lying on the ground. See an old wooden cot…grey blankets." He is aware of a deep sadness, it seems that this man bitterly regrets his actions but it is too late.

"What was he meant to learn?" I question him.

"He didn't learn what he was supposed to learn…to be kind. He didn't let his heart open up."

"What beliefs have you carried over from this experience into your current life?"

"Trust," he says simply. "Learn to trust." He understands the lesson now, and I ask him to let the connection with his partner take him to a previous lifetime together.

"Outside a large brown house, close to the street," he says immediately. "Brown bricks, white bricks around the outside of the windows…large front door. Big heavy oak door, white bricks around." He is quiet for a while, reflective.

"What are you feeling as you stand there?"

"Sadness. Looks like a wealthy person's house…sadness inside."

"What is the source of the sadness?"

"We are friends…he's dying," he says simply. I ask him to describe his friend. "Tall, slim, dark hair…bit gangly," he chuckles to himself. "Silly…does stupid things…he's just crazy, dumb, ungainly!" He laughs again and it is a pleasure to see his face light up with the memory. "Makes me laugh all the time…he just does things…it doesn't matter. He's funny looking…tall and skinny, I'm a bit shy. He's always popular, calls me his best friend." His expression changes quickly. "He's dying…he's been hurt…don't know how…wrapped in bandages on his chest. Doctor said there's nothing more they can do…maid is crying. I just stand there, don't know what to say, I don't want him to go. I sit on the bed and hold his hand…he's pale and grey. I'm desperate for him to stay…he's not going to." There is a pause and he seems deeply distressed, then adds, "He says it's ok, he's all right…little smile. I just stare at him; just keep thinking I don't know how to live after this. I just thought…I was living through him…he just dies." He is hardly breathing, the pain of loss is so intense and I want to bring his attention to what is happening in his body, where he holds on.

"In my chest…throat…stomach," he tells me. This is the inner core of our body and it is no surprise that he has held onto all his painful emotions there, this is quite common. Often people carry excess weight around that area of their body as they try to compensate by filling that deep hole with food or drink. I ask him for any last thoughts or feelings surrounding this experience.

"I go home…never get another friend again," he says sadly. "I don't want to feel like this ever again."

Here is the key to his problems; he has closed his heart down to avoid being hurt again. I ask him what he feels he needs to learn from this experience.

"It's ok to love," he smiles. "It's ok to like people, but if they hurt you, you don't have to shut them out. It's ok to be unhappy for a little bit," he acknowledges, "they didn't mean it…forgiveness is important."

"You can release the sadness from these other lifetimes now," I tell him. "You can choose to open your heart and release the pain."

He lays there quietly for a while as his unconscious does what it needs to do and brings back some new awareness with him.

"When my friend died, I didn't forgive him for leaving," he admits, "and before that, the old man – he knew he had done wrong, that's why they left. He was faced with the consequences of his actions…crushed by them, by the pointlessness of it all."

He leaves determined to live his life fully, and comforted by the fact that he and his partner will have other lifetimes together as soul mates. His karmic pathway reading confirms that he needs to step out from the shadow of his partner and embrace life fully in his own right.

CHAPTER 5
Annabelle's story

In my work with people, some of the most painful learning experiences have been in the arena of relationships. Why they are often so difficult, even with those that we love, is a constant source of anguish for many. In our family relationships the lessons can be especially difficult; absent or abusive parents, abandonment and betrayals are common themes. As we become adults, we seem to grasp onto the idea of soul mates, believing that if we could only 'find the right one,' then everything will come right in our lives. Regression work teaches us that often the opposite is true. The ones that we love the most are here to help us learn the hardest lessons. The following story may help to illustrate this.

During the life between lifetimes, three souls, bonded by love, met to discuss their next incarnation together.
"I want to learn something really valuable in this next life," said Soul 1.
"I will give you the gifts of independence and resilience so that you can develop the strength of purpose to fulfil your destiny," said Soul 2.
"And I will give you the gifts of patience and compassion which you will need if you are to follow your soul's calling," said Soul 3.
Soul 1 was thrilled! "These are great gifts indeed," she cried. "I accept with gratitude."
"But wait," added Soul 2, "there is a condition. In order to receive the gifts of independence and resilience you will feel abandoned by me for much of your adult life."
"And in order to receive my gifts of patience and compassion," said Soul 3, "you will also be angry with me and feel betrayed for much of your adult life."
Soul 1 was horrified. "How can I knowingly accept these gifts if it will cause so much pain?" she asked.
Souls 2 and 3 conferred for a while and then said: "We have an additional gift which will help you-we will give you the gift of forgetting until you remember your soul's purpose."

So, in time, the three souls incarnated together, Souls 2 and 3 as parents to Soul 1. The harder Soul 1 tried to get close to her emotionally distant mother, the more busy she became, until she felt so alone that she gave up trying to do anything with her at all and just did things by herself. She became so angry with her father who was always ill and afraid of everything in life, that she carried that frustration with her into her adult relationships with men.
And so Soul 1 learned to become resilient and independent from an early age, and, in time, went on to become a patient and compassionate healer who helped many lost souls find their purpose.
Then, one day, she woke up, realised that she was indeed fulfilling her soul's true purpose in this lifetime and remembered the contract that she had made so long ago. In place of the bitterness, she was finally able to feel grateful to have had parents who enabled her to develop those very qualities that she needed.

It can be helpful to ask ourselves what qualities we developed from those early, painful experiences and to see them as gifts that are essential for us to follow our soul's purpose. Although it is sometimes difficult to understand why we have to choose such hard lessons to learn what we are meant to learn, what better way could you learn about self empowerment than by being disempowered? Self love through being rejected? Inner strength through being abandoned? It's a cosmic joke isn't it! Letting go of blame, forgiving others and taking responsibility for moving our own lives forward frees us to be all that we can be and gives us the joy of knowing that there is a higher purpose that we can believe in. The following stories demonstrate how letting go of these difficult emotions in a positive way allowed those involved to move on with their lives, as well as helping them to evolve spiritually.

Annabelle's story

Annabelle came for a regression looking for closure with someone in her life with whom she had been intimately connected. The relationship had not worked out and was a source of angst for her. Recently married, she now wanted to get on with her life and put the pain of the past behind her. I had known Annabelle for some time and knew that she trusted me. To my mind, this is a very important factor in a successful regression as the individual is able to let go more easily, thus allowing them a deeper experience in many cases.

Very quickly she entered a deep state as evidenced by the rolling of her eyes under her lids, and I knew immediately that she was one of those individuals who could 'see' a whole movie under hypnosis. Only a relatively small percentage of people that I have regressed are able to go into such a deep state so quickly.
It was Christmas in England she said; she could see their Christmas tree. She began to laugh.
"What is so funny?" I asked her curiously.
"The dog!" she giggled. "He's eaten all the little chocolates off it and spat out the wrappers! Mum's there....there's all bits of tin foil on the floor that the dog spat out." I left her there for a few moments to enjoy this memory at her leisure before regressing her back to an earlier age.

"I'm watching TV in my nursery," she said finally, "on a little chair. I'm falling backwards off the chair but I'm ok, scared but just winded. I'm watching Policeman Pat, there's a butterfly picture on the wall." She was silent for a moment or two then her eyes started to move more rapidly as though she was tracking something. "I'm lying in my cot, there's a mobile hanging over it, scarecrow in the middle, four animals, pig sheep, horse and cow." She had regressed to an earlier memory so quickly that she had caught me by surprise. "The mobile seems big and bright," she commented, "but I don't like the room." There seemed nothing more so I decided to try regressing her to a time when she had a connection with the person she had come about.

"Medieval castle," she said straight away. "Very big, very old. In a nursery with a nanny or wet nurse, rocking horse, real horse's hair." The words tumbled out and I marveled at the speed and the detail in which she was able to recount what she was seeing. "There's a real fire," she added, "not many other children, one other and a baby. I'm wearing a long dark red dress. I can go outside, nicer outside. I have a brother; he's frightened of the water, big fountain in the garden." Her head moved restlessly and she was quiet for a while. I wondered if something had happened to him and just as I was trying to decide whether to ask her (I was very conscious of not wanting to lead her) she said, "he fell in the fountain, it made him frightened of the water. He's thin, pale...sickly kind of child. Have to look after him a bit," she added helpfully. I asked her how that was for her, to have to look after him. "It's OK," she said. "The children are related, but one of the parents is different, the father is different...me and my brother have the same father."
A pause and then, "I'm getting older, have to dress up more, doing sewing, pricking myself with the needle." Suddenly she exclaimed in surprise "My soul mate is my brother! He has to go away...school...boarding house," she frowned at the memory. "The girls don't go - only the boy goes." I asked her how that was for her. "its ok,' she reflected, "he

writes… bad handwriting…letters don't come very often. Comes back once. He's taller, very anxious, doesn't like being away, still scared of the water." I remembered her telling me at the beginning of the session that she felt very responsible for the friend who was the reason for her regression and it was apparent that she felt the same responsibility for her brother in this past life.

She continued with her story. "I go away somewhere, on a ship…moving…long time on the ship, can feel the movement of it. Going to some other country with a man, not my brother-he can't come," she explains. "I have to go, it's Egypt. My husband digs…he's interested in digging up things. I like looking at them too, but not as much as him. It's hot and dry here. My brother…I miss him," she adds wistfully. "We leave there eventually, back to a different house in England, it's so green!" she exclaims, adding "it's a long journey. My husband brings back crates of relics. We're back on the ship again…same bad weather." She sighs, "we get through it." There is a period of quiet and I leave her there to process whatever is happening, knowing that she will tell me when she is ready.

"I'm back in England," she tells me suddenly. "My brother's in gaol…don't know what for." She is silent for quite a while. "What happens to him?" I ask her eventually "He dies, she says quietly, sounding very sad. "He gets an infection. I see him coughing up blood, it's cold and dark and damp. I'm at his funeral now."

I wonder if she feels responsible for his death, seeing a potential link back to the friend in her current life, and so I ask her.

"What do you tell yourself about his death?"

"I'm surprised that he lived to this age," she replies. "Part of me knows the connection was different, stronger, now it's gone. I see myself alone a lot, don't go back. My husband gets more crates. I never have that connection again." I ask her if there is any way that she feels responsible for what happened to her brother. "I promised him to help him get over his water thing, but it's too deep to fix," she adds. "I can't help him, he's too scared. He was only young when he fell in, was with me, nanny was there. I saw him fall in, scared himself…crying…came out cold, wasn't in long…big fuss made. I don't feel responsible now, wish I could teach him to swim but he was too scared." She accepts that there is nothing else she could have done.

Finally, she goes to her own death at my suggestion and sees herself giving birth. "It's taking too long…doctor there, nothing they can do…baby's all right," she tells me, "but I don't die straight away, too much blood." I ask her if she recognizes the baby now, still wondering about a possible connection with someone in this life, but she shakes her head. "It's ok; I know the baby will get looked after." We leave it there and I take her to the life between lives, called the bardo state by the Tibetans, to establish what the lessons are that she was meant to learn from these experiences. She makes the following associations for herself:

"Will have time to be powerful…have power over others…position of power."

"What are you meant to learn with your brother?" I ask her

"Life isn't permanent," she tells me. "We don't have to be physically with someone to have a connection with them."

"What needs to happen with your soul mate in this life?" I ask her, wanting to help her clear any unwanted emotional charge attached to the experience.

To my surprise, instead of coming back, her eyes begin to move again as she goes to another memory.

"Crowd of people, trying to get somewhere. I'm holding on to his hands, the force of the crowd is pushing us in opposite directions. I can't find him, can't see him. He will end up alone, but I'm not…" Her words peter out. "He will be vulnerable. I'm with everyone else and he got separated from us."

"What happens to him?" I ask gently.

She continues on as if she doesn't hear me and says, "I can't understand how I can't see him, but I can't! I keep looking for him, hoping he will come back, but I don't find him." She is distressed and I tell her to go to this life and understand the link, what is important for her to know and understand.

"He still can't swim," she says sadly. "I can't save him. He still makes the same mistakes. I can let him go to learn his own lessons, with compassion," she realizes.

I move to reassure her. "You will meet again in other lifetimes."

We go on to discuss the concept of people returning across lifetimes to clear old karmic patterns. Sometimes, individuals are just not ready or able to learn the lesson and we talk about the possibility of them being reunited in some future life when perhaps he may be ready and able to take responsibility for himself. What was important was that she recognized that it was not her failure. There was nothing more that she could have done to help him, he had to help himself.

On follow up, Annabelle told me that the emotional charge attached to this person had cleared. She now no longer found herself thinking and worrying about him and was relieved to have peace around her past. I was very pleased to have been able to help her as she is very special to me, I suspect not just from this lifetime but from previous ones where I believe that I contracted to assist her in this life with her life's purpose.

The way that we met spoke of a karmic connection. At a professional dinner that ordinarily, neither of us would bother to have attended, we found ourselves seated next to each other at the end of the table, which gave us an opportunity to have a more private discussion. There was an immediate sense of connection and we began talking about spiritual journeys, and so began our friendship.

Often, when individuals come for counseling about soul mate relationships, there is angst or conflict involved. There is a popular belief that one has only one soul mate which puts intense pressure on us to "find them, and make it work." My personal belief is that although that may certainly be true in some cases, there are other kinds of soul connections, all of them designed to teach us something important or take us in a particular direction.

My first husband was the catalyst in my leaving England and coming over to Australia. It was a very tortuous and emotionally traumatic relationship for me, but I am so thankful for the experience, as it took my life in a very different direction which ultimately led to my being able to pursue my life's work, as well as giving me a beautiful son from that union. I have no doubts that if I had stayed in England, I would not have been able, because of my family circumstances, to pursue my spiritual path. We cannot always be aware of the significance of an event at the time it happens; this is where trusting our intuition becomes so very crucial. When a soul call comes, you have to go by instinct and you have to be brave without knowing what the end result will be. If I had not trusted mine, I would never have gone to America to be trained by Brian Weiss and this book would never have been written.

CHAPTER 6
Pauline's story

Pauline's story is a prime example of how karmic relationships can exert their influence across lifetimes. Often, there is a sense of having 'been there before' when the same experience occurs again, bringing with it all the tears and anguish which seem so familiar to the person experiencing them.

Her story was one of the most intriguing regressions I have ever had the pleasure of conducting, perhaps even more so because she found it very difficult to relax during the whole process. Initially hesitant to approach me, she expressed an interest in exploring what she felt was a 'block' which was stopping her from moving forward in her life. She wondered if regression work might help her get to 'the root' of the problem.

I agreed although, privately, I did wonder how open she would be to hypnosis, given that she described herself as 'a bit of a control freak' who tended to be overly analytical in her orientation to life. As hypnosis relies to some degree on the subject's ability to let go and be open to whatever they experience, this could represent a significant difficulty. Nevertheless, she was keen to try and so we scheduled a time for her to make the long drive to see me.

During our first session together, she told me a little more about herself. I find background information very useful as it often acts as a bridge between the person's current life and the karmic lessons that come up during the regression. In Pauline's case, she described feeling 'paralyzed' in her life and 'unable to act on her own behalf.' She had left her partner when their son was two years old and talked of 'slogging along alone' for 26 years. "Sometimes," she added, she felt "split down the middle," as though there were two of her. All this was very interesting background, but, as was normal, I had no way of knowing where this experience was going or how relevant it would be.

Although I made Pauline as comfortable as I could and did an extra long induction, as I expected, she found it very hard to relax and suspend judgment about what she was experiencing. At one stage she even opened her eyes and said (with some frustration!) that maybe she was just making it all up in her head! I asked her where she was, to establish whether she had been able to let go of her current surroundings and, sounding puzzled, she said it seemed just like a big empty, dark space to her. She was wandering around and the word 'abandoned' kept coming into her mind but nothing else was becoming clear to her. At this point I was also beginning to feel that perhaps we should just give up on this attempt, nevertheless I reassured her as best I could and encouraged her to let go of any expectations that she might have of herself. This seemed to help and after a while her breathing slowed down and she sighed.

Another stretch of time elapsed before she suddenly sat up and said she needed to go to the toilet. As she disappeared down the hallway, I was aware of a feeling of disappointment that she had not got what she wanted from the experience. However, both of us were in for a big surprise!

On her return, she almost ran back into the office and, in great excitement, told me that while she was sitting on the toilet, (inspiration comes in the strangest places!), she heard a voice in her head say, quite distinctly, 'of course it was abandoned, it is the ballroom of an old abandoned castle!' She went on to explain that she somehow just knew this old castle was surrounded by huge gardens that she used to wander in. At the same time, her conscious analytical mind remained skeptical about the experience, but she still wanted to make another appointment. What happened next time was even more surprising.

She settled into a relaxed state a little more easily but still found it difficult to stop her conscious mind from judging. However, as she reported a sensation of being held from behind, she 'felt' that it was a man and that he had a knife. "I was killed there, at the castle!" she added in disbelief. Again, we had another toilet break, her conscious mind seemed hell bent on taking control (or perhaps it was her bladder!). When she returned, she was again eager to talk about the experience.

I asked her how she had died and she told me, quite indignantly, that he had stabbed her from behind, holding her with his left arm and stabbing her with his right hand. "So, he would have stabbed you on the left breast if he was right handed," I mused aloud. "Yes!" she exclaimed, "right where I have that pain in my chest, but it can't have been that…" At this point she began poking at her chest on the left side to show me where the pain was, at the same time telling me that the pain had been there for years. To her disbelief, it was gone, she was unable to find it no matter how much she poked and prodded. (I had no prior knowledge of this pain before the regression as she had not mentioned it).

Two months later, I received a letter from her. The persistent and very sharp pain that she had experienced had disappeared. Later, she recalled having a man's hand placed over her mouth, as though to silence her and her sense was that this was her former husband, the father of her son. As had happened before, other information filtered through to her soon after her session, and when she drove away that day, she had a really strong feeling that she had been pregnant and that the child she was carrying was her son in this life.

Later that evening, still feeling quite emotional, she began to share the story with her son. At this point he was interested, she said, but not emotionally involved with the story. When she put her hand up to her mouth and explained that she felt that she had been "gagged", he gave a gasp and his eyes welled up with tears. He then felt very connected to the story and there was a real sense that he had experienced it too. Her feeling was that his father had deprived them of a life together and that this time around, he has been deprived of a life with his son, and perhaps her, because she had left him when her son was only two years old. She felt there was a strong sense of karmic justice in how events had turned out and was able to go and live her life freed of the old guilt and without the physical pain which had troubled her for so many years.

It is always a great pleasure for me when clients can go on to live the rest of their lives freed of pain and with a greater understanding and belief in the spiritual aspect of life. Pauline's experience also reminded me that clients use different sensory modalities to process information, and for a 'feeler' like Pauline, it was quite difficult to visually 'see' anything in a regression. Feeling was her dominant way of processing information and so, in hindsight, it was logical that her experience came to her in that way. This information was very valuable for me in reminding me to use language which reflected the person's preferred sensory mode during the relaxation process.

CHAPTER 7
David's story

David had an intense fear of abandonment in relationships. Fearful of betrayal, he found it hard to trust his partner enough to be able to move forward in their relationship and had come hoping that the answer lay somewhere in a past life. Trapped in a job for which he had little enthusiasm, he also felt stuck in his own life with respect to his soul's purpose. I decided to try some initial visualisation exercises with him to loosen him up before taking him to the doorway of his own house.

"Front door…red federation brick…clay pavers…mat. See motorbike parked over there…car's close by. Wooden gate…timberwork…daytime. Can see front gate…plants in pots on side." We progressed with no trouble to his roof top.
"On top of roof. See neighbours properties, big tree, shed, paving, new house behind me, air conditioner, patio, other neighbour's citrus trees, plants."
"Turn 360 degrees and tell me what you see."
"See lots of trees…old tree dead…very high…not a stump." He is very specific about the detail which tells me that he is able to visualise very clearly.
"Can you change this scene to night time?" I ask him.
He could. "Moon reflecting off roof of house behind…very bright light…reflecting strongly…warm…can see streetlights."
By now I am satisfied that he is relaxed enough to go into a deeper experience and lead him to an early childhood memory.
"In playground…primary school…brown shoes…about six or seven, standing in line, waiting for dancing class, nothing fancy or formal, feel excited. He describes a little of his enjoyment of dancing and new experiences before going to an earlier memory. It appeared to be a happy time for him.
"Me - little blanket…comfort." He is unable to talk much, consistent with his regression age and I decide to hone in on the reason for his visit.
"Go to the source of the problem in your current life, to a time when you experienced abandonment and betrayal."
"Very long time ago…air is clear… bright blue sky. I'm in a garden…see my feet…leather sandals. Weird – I'm wearing a dress!" He quickly recovers from his surprise. "Pleated…roman type outfit…not a dress," he emphasises, somewhat hastily. "I'm physically very strong. Not sure this is where I wanted to be," he says suddenly, seeming uncomfortable.
"Just trust and go with it," I tell him, knowing that the connection is not always apparent straight away.
"Think its Egypt. I'm a soldier of some kind. I'm at peace with myself. Very fit…athletic."
"He is proud of his body," I affirm.
"Yes. He has confidence in himself…no doubts, he's a leader. I'm supposed to meet somebody there…they haven't shown up…a woman."
"Do you know why she hasn't shown up?"
"We have been discovered!" His body stiffens and his expression appears fearful. "We are in love…forbidden…she is somebody else's partner…strong feelings for her. Same woman I am with now." Later, he tells me that this is the

only possible relationship for him. Because of his position, he is always moving on. However, this relationship is still forbidden, and now he must reap the consequences.

"Can you move this story forward like a movie?" I ask him. "What happens to her?…to you?

"I can't see her…I'm thrown off a cliff!" He is outraged, in disbelief that this could happen to him, a soldier in the prime of his life.

"What are your last thoughts?" I ask him.

"How did they know? I'm not ready to go." That much is evident; he is still having trouble accepting what has happened to him, shaking his head in denial. Finally, he accepts the reality of it.

"Sadness…she couldn't be with me. She won't let go."

Afterwards, we discuss the connection between his current relationship and the one from back then.

"It is possible that you had a karmic contract to find each other again in this life," I explain to him. "It was a forbidden relationship back then, so perhaps there is some residual guilt on her part too." He has noticed some ambivalence on her part about their current relationship, and I wonder if it is a forbidden one in this life too.

"You can only be responsible for your own thoughts and actions," I tell him gently. "Even though you feel you are meant to be together, we can not be responsible for someone else's growth or decisions, just be all you can be in this life and be open to the possibility. The abandonment you experienced back then was compounded by the fact that you were in the prime of your life, fit, happy and with a lot to look forward to. There are some parallels with your current life-perhaps being fit, happy and successful now brings up the fear that it will all be taken away from you?" I question him.

He agrees that yes, he is extremely committed to his fitness routine and proud of his body.

"If she is meant to be with you, the opportunity is there to resolve any unfinished business," I reassure him.

I had noticed a parallel between the overly harsh judgement of himself in this life and the previous life, and ask him, "Is it possible that you also judged yourself harshly for entering into a 'wrong' relationship with her which may have contributed to her death or punishment?" He concedes that this is possible and briefly acknowledges the pain that living outside of one's values can cause.

Later, he showed me a draft of a manuscript that he had written and asked for my comments. I was impressed by the wisdom and insights reflected in his writing and encouraged him to find a publisher. This was evidently an old soul; perhaps his regression would be the catalyst that helped him to connect with his soul's purpose, I hoped so for his sake.

PERSONAL NOTES

Inner Alchemy

SECTION 3

EMOTIONAL HEALING

CHAPTER 8
Bonnie's story

The emotional healing that comes from regression work is profound. There is something about re-experiencing events in an emotional context that allows the body to release the pain of those events. It is different to mere imagination or the telling of a story which can occur in a relatively detached way. The intensity of the emotions which accompany the re telling of an event is often an indicator of the length of time and the depth at which these feelings have been buried.

Many of those who come for regression are seeking happiness in the form of answers to questions or resolution to particular problems that they might be experiencing. It takes enormous effort to hold in the emotional impact of distressing events and I believe that this is one of the reasons that our society is experiencing depression on such a large scale. Imagine that holding being compounded across lifetimes and it is then easy to understand the enormity of the karmic load that we carry.

Emotional release also occurs in other ways. I have had clients laugh their way through a regression at memories that amuse them and others who have been astonished or highly motivated by what they have witnessed. Given a supportive space, the body will find the most appropriate way to release pent up emotions and the relief that follows is immense. The following stories indicate the depth of emotional healing that can come from regression work.

Betrayal is a common theme in regression work, and revisiting past life experiences with this theme can help to clarify relationship difficulties and the inherent karmic contracts. At the time of her visit, Bonnie had some very serious custody issues with her former partner. Having become pregnant after a relatively short liaison, she found that her ex partner was unwilling to let go of his unborn child after the relationship had ended. Frustrated, anxious and afraid to stand her ground, she sought a regression in the hopes that it might shed some light on his continued unwelcome presence in her life. Having worked with me before, she very quickly entered a deep trance state, as evidenced by her deep breathing and rapid eye movements.

"I'm in France. He wanted to take me to the castle…gates locked. It's after hours so we went for a walk along the stone walls." I wonder if it is her current lifetime, knowing that they had holidayed there. She pauses, her eyes still moving rapidly.

"We are climbing over the wall, can see a European forest of oak and beech trees. He (her ex partner) begins to tell me the story of the castle. It's Arthur's castle…round table…Arthur…lover…betrayal. Amazing scene, Lady of the Lake is there…tall tower to the left…extraordinary scene!" Her voice is full of wonder. I let go of trying to understand which time she is in now and wait for the story to unfold, knowing that any interruptions will only pull her off track.

"There's a tower…I'm going up to the door…can hear voices and sounds…maybe pigeons or birds?" She frowns, unsure it seems. "It sounded like the place was alive-I know what I am going to see in the tower!" she exclaims suddenly. "I'm looking up, the steps are rotted away but we are going up there." She expresses her delight looking up to the top. "It's vibrating with energy! I'm excited to be here," and then, just as suddenly, she wants to get out of there. "Vision of big log fire…people in costume," she says quickly. "He wants me to climb the stairs to the top of the tower." She doesn't want to go now.

"Come on – trust me!" he says.

"In myself, I thought -NO!" she tells me. "Looking at him… it's a test…I will be betrayed!" she says suddenly, "most powerful feeling…"

Nevertheless, she says nothing of her misgivings and they go up the stairwell.

"There's a hole…door missing…void below. My heart's pumping," she adds and, indeed, her chest reflects her rapid breathing as the cellular memory rises. "I'm pregnant," she tells me. I am still not sure whether she is in her current life or a past life or both, but let go of trying to understand, knowing that the important thing is that she will make sense of it for herself.

She is uncomfortable, full of fear, hearing a voice in her head. "Get out of here!" it tells her, but almost irrevocably, she is drawn to follow him to the top.

"I'm numb… almost frozen with fear… slit window…wrought iron gate. We're stopping now. He wants me to climb up. "No!" I tell him.

"It will be fine." He is insistent that she follow him.

"Didn't want him to be there…I watched him climb with complete hatred. He's wrong…can't believe I'm pregnant to him! Something hits me on the temple…ancient nail…an arrow…turned my head…fell on the ground…hit me."

The past life memory flashes in front of her -they have been together before. "How much more of a wake up do I need?" She is horrified. "Want to go-right now. Did I tell him? Is it worth telling him? I wonder." She seems unable to tell him about her experience, how she is feeling. "We're walking down now…little spiral stone staircase. He pauses then says, "let's go through this way."

I'm angry, want to get out. Finally, he respects my wishes.

"I knew I shouldn't have trusted you!" It just came out of my mouth.

Finally, she is able to tell him her thoughts, and quickly he flies into a jealous rage, accusing her of not having got over her former love. Her heart is thumping in her chest and now her fears seem justified, but she is already trapped, pregnant to him. Her inner voice continues to warn her, "get the hell away from this guy-he's dangerous, loose."

"But I'm pregnant to him," she argues back.

"Need to run for your life from this guy. How much do you need before you can run away?" Her intuition tells her she is in danger.

She does leave him before the baby is born, but now they are irrevocably bound together through parenthood, he will not let go of his child. She is resigned to the fact that there are karmic lessons that still need to be learned from each other and it seems they are destined to work it out in this lifetime, but now she knows that she has to speak up to protect both herself and her daughter. She is calm, resolute. Reliving the experience, which actually did occur during their short time together, and the embedded past life memory which came out of it, confirmed her fears about the relationship. He betrayed her before and would not respect her wishes in this lifetime either. He is intent on getting his own way.

This past life memory fragment was particularly powerful for her. It enabled her to see the truth of the situation and find her inner strength in order to be able to speak up and deal assertively with him. My sense is that only when they are able to deal respectfully and openly with each other will this karmic connection be fully healed. This of course is the conundrum-we cannot influence how or whether someone else chooses to learn their own lessons, but we can choose how we deal with the impact of those experiences on ourselves.

CHAPTER 9
Janie's story

Guilt is what we do to ourselves in our thoughts when we are not at peace in our minds with something that we have done or not done, however it is one of the most devastating feelings to deal with. Insidious and relentless, people often use words like 'eating away at me,' and 'paralysing' to describe the effects on their psyche. Our subconscious is so powerful that it can take these destructive messages and translate them into actual physical illnesses like cancer and restrictions in the body. It doesn't distinguish between 'right' or 'wrong' messages but merely works to manifest our thoughts into experience.

Janie's story illustrates beautifully the freedom that results when guilt is released at a subconscious level from cellular memory. Her story is followed by several others who struggled with the same feeling before finally becoming free of it through their regression experiences.
An attractive woman in her early to mid forties, Janie was shortly leaving Australia to live in Europe, (a long cherished dream of hers) with her partner. She requested help in resolving her feelings of overwhelming guilt about leaving her daughter behind, which was spoiling her anticipation of this exciting new life. They were very close, having been on their own since the break up of her marriage. She also suffered from frequent head spinning and brain fogginess, particularly when under stress emotionally.

She was excited about the idea of a regression, and shortly after the induction, was breathing slowly and rhythmically. I asked her to go to a childhood memory which was connected in some way with her symptoms and soon her eyelids began flickering, an indication that she was visually re-experiencing.
"What do you become aware of?"
"I'm with a friend in England…didn't come home for tea. We caught the bus… maybe a train, we're a long way from home." She pauses and frowns. "I'm in trouble from mum and dad…frightened because I knew I was going to cop it from dad. Don't know why we did it (another pause)…maybe just to see what it was like to be free." At this point she becomes tearful. "I'm only little…mum and dad couldn't show their feelings." She quickly moves between past and present and has no trouble going to another memory when asked.
"I'm two years old…waiting for dad at end of the drive…he put me on the crossbar of his bike…nice." She smiles. Doing something with me, I'm wearing a little frilly dress…never felt very pretty," she explains, "just trying to please." I ask her whether she wants to remain with this memory and she shakes her head 'no,' so I make a suggestion that she can go back as far as she wishes to find another memory that is relevant to her current situation.
She is quiet for a while and then begins to move her head from side to side and I ask her to go into her body and let the memory come from that. Often I find that going into a particular body sensation can serve as a cue for the memory, and sure enough, straight away she begins to describe her surroundings.
"I'm wearing a pilgrim dress, all black…have really long hair." She pauses for a moment. "In a little wooden house, no one else there…can feel someone, wrenching my head back with my ponytail…can't see who it is. I fall down backwards…am being dragged by my ponytail, feel it in my head and neck…being out of control, trying to not be pulled." There is a long pause, and then she continues. "Still happening…man…image of rough hands…I have upset

him." She jumps back to describing the house using staccato like phrases as though she doesn't want to waste too much time there. "Spartan wood shack…no rugs on floor...bare boards...very basic. It's night time.", she adds helpfully.

As the experience is quite violent which is at odds with the calmness of her voice, I ask her how she is feeling. "Wondering what's going to happen…" She pauses; "I have got up now…room is empty…man gone. Door is ajar… can see outside… nothing to see." She frowns, "must have been someone I knew. My neck is ok, hair has been pulled and scalp is tingling. I am wearing a black dress with a high neck, tight bodice, long sleeves, in my 20's."

I ask her what she is doing there and she replies as though she is surprised by the question "I'm just there." Trying to find out more, I ask her if it is her house. "Yes, familiar…not very homely, doesn't look like a couples house. I see an old brick fireplace, black cooking pot over the fire. Outside the door there's a big trough…my head has been in it!" she exclaims suddenly. "Can feel where my head has been pressed down, trough is pressing there on my collar bone." She touches her collar bone, showing me. "Aware of strong workman's hands again…can feel my heart beating hard. Got boot things on…making marks on the ground...pushing to get free. Not afraid…just want to be free…don't want it…it feels like it is not unusual. Can feel it pulling on my neck...not comfortable...cold...can feel the water is really cold..." Her body shivers. "Feeling it (coldness) in my head. I am unhappy, unloved and abused…dark environment… no light." She describes the outside as an extension of the Spartan wooden cabin. Suddenly she tenses and I sense we are getting to the part that contains the emotional charge for her.

"She has a sister - something happened to her! Just know it! We used to be close…she is younger, real pretty, little bonnet…needs to smile but never does. She dies at ten or eleven years old…a hard life," she adds sadly. "My hands are red and chill blainy looking…do lots of work, chopping wood, washing and things. My name or my sister's name is Caroline. I want to be happy," she adds fiercely. "Go where the sun shines."

"What stops you?"

"Circumstances," she replies. "Dismal place…feel trapped…like a prisoner. Just there…forced to put up with the abuse. I'm just there." The last words are said in a resigned voice, that's her fate as she sees it. "That man is….he's just evil….darkened room…just out of the light. Can see parts of his clothing…brown coloured wool coat to knees, boots and workman's trousers, big belly and waistcoat. Can't see his face."

"What is his relationship to you?" I ask.

"Thinks he has a right to me," she adds, sounding bitter. "Not my husband…repulsed by him, he's horrible!" She screws up her face in seeming disgust. "Want to be with people…don't want to be there. Not married…no rings. Hurts where he's pressed down on my collar bone."

As she seems in some discomfort, I ask her to release the memory now from her body and suggest that she no longer has to feel those sensations in her neck. I take her to the garden and allow time for her guides and helpers to communicate the reasons behind this miserable life she has relived today then ask her if she is aware of the lessons she is meant to learn from this experience.

"To experience suffering in a past life and appreciate a good one. Knowing that you can have a happier time later-not all lifetimes are like that," she answers confidently.

"She can have a happier life?" I confirm.

"Yes. She can enjoy this life and know that she deserves it." She adds that her daughter was her sister in this past life, and that she felt guilty for not being able to help her. This helps to ease the guilt that she feels at leaving her daughter behind.

"I feel really light now," she tells me, her face shining with joy, and I am pleased for her.

I reinforce the fact that she is free to choose now and summarise the learning from the reliving of these experiences for her.

"There is no need now to please someone else at the expense of yourself, you are free to enjoy your good life now and knowing that you deserve it means that you can release the guilt you feel about leaving your daughter. Your karmic pathway also suggests that you need to be away on your own and be free to develop your spiritual pathway. Enjoy it!"

She smiles and as she leaves, her relief is obvious. I hear later from her daughter that she does leave to live in Europe and is very happy. She is free of the dreadful guilt at last, and her daughter is happy for her.

CHAPTER 10
Linda's story

Linda was a very attractive woman who was plagued with insecurities about not being 'good enough.' She worked in the health and beauty field and showed a great commitment to her work and to her clients, often to her own detriment. She would routinely push herself to the point of exhaustion in order to keep up with her commitments to her partner, children and clients, and found it hard to refuse any request made of her.
Linda had been attending counselling and was interested in regression as a way to investigate the possible causes of her insecurities with the hope of gaining some relief from her need 'to be all things to all people.'
As we began to prepare for her regression, she commented that she had not one actual memory of her childhood, only the sense of not being noticed as a child. Quite quickly after inducting her, she told me that she could see a house.

"I'm playing in the garden, I'm a really happy little kid, just not noticed," she explained. It became apparent straight away that her outside image did not match her internal state. "I look happy but inside I'm so frustrated I could scream!" she tells me. "I just want to know why-just want to stamp my foot but I have nothing to complain about, none of us do, we have a good life." She is at a loss to explain her feelings. She thinks she is about ten years old then and I take her back earlier.
"Lots of children," she tells me, "I'm poor, pretty lucky with a family though. We live in a little village with horses, wheels, wagons and lots of children! I have brown clothes on, old clothes…very worn. It's cold," she shivers, pulling the blanket up around her and I quickly put another one over her feet.
"It's England," she explains, "lots of little kids, (she seems bemused by this) not many girls," she adds. "We're stuck in a street…not dirt…pebbles. The kids are following a cart." I ask her why, sensing that this might be important. "So we don't get left behind." She frowns and adds, "the people in the cart only want the boys because they work hard. I see me; I'm little, three to four years old…really, really pretty…long white blond curly hair. I get to go but only because I'm pretty. I have to be happy or I don't get to go."
She emphasizes this point, wanting me to understand the importance of it. "If I'm happy and pretty, I get to go. They can't get rid of all the girls." She is silent for a while, seeming to ponder this and so I ask her if she is aware of the purpose of this life. "I don't know," she says at first and then on reflection, "be happy so everyone wants me around. It's ok if I'm happy, I smile at people, they smile back. I sing lots and they come and hug me, it makes them feel better, makes me feel happy."
The connection between her current problems with insecurity and this life seem apparent and I ask her if she wants to go to any other life that might be relevant. "No," she replies straight away and almost immediately moves into another experience in the same lifetime. Despite her reluctance, there is more of this story to come.
"I'm ashamed," she whispers. "I'm working the streets…a prostitute. The same girl, but grown up. Everybody still likes me, I'm still pretty…live quite well, not in flash houses, still on the streets. I don't like what I do, but it still makes everyone happy." I feel sad for her, seeing all too well the trap that she is in and question her gently:
"What do you tell yourself about this experience?"
"I've got nothing to complain about," she says stoically. "There are people worse off than me. I can walk down the streets; everyone says hello to me…smiles at me." She pauses for a moment and then adds, "don't think some of the women do." She becomes emotional and begins to cry softly. "They don't talk to me. I don't really need them," she

says angrily. "There are plenty of people there to talk to-I'm just the same as them!" She changes tack abruptly again. It's as though she is fighting with herself.

"I shouldn't be here, I'm better than this! I should be in one of the posh houses, none of the men there love me-why am I still here?" she wails. "I've got nothing to complain about, I should be happy. I don't mind sex, I actually love the people but I feel ashamed because it's wrong." She seems very conflicted about her role in this life, constantly trying to justify her choice. Finally she admits the truth to herself. "I should have one man who makes me happy-I'm going to burn in hell!" I remember that she has been brought up in a very strict religious family and I quickly remind her that she had limited choices.

Finally the realisation hits her. "I came from an orphanage! That's where I grew up." Suddenly all her previous comments about having to be happy and look pretty make sense. I move to reassure her.

"You had no one else; you did what you had to do to survive. You worked with what you have got; if you're pretty and happy, everyone wants you," I remind her.

She argues with me. "I should hate what I'm doing but it makes me feel good to think all those people like me. I want to be in a big house of my own." Finally she begins to accept it. "I did what I had to do," but she is still conflicted. "I try so hard to be there (in the big houses) but I'm not really good enough. I don't like what I do; I know deep inside of me it's wrong. People that pay for me don't love me…I know inside I shouldn't be doing it. I want to be the good girl…good soul and good heart."

We conclude here and I spend some time reassuring her again that she did what she had to do to survive and that in this life now, she has more choices available to her. She can decide what is right for her instead of having to please everyone. She accepts the truth of this but the restrictions of her religious upbringing weigh heavily on her. She tells me that she is currently ostracized by her own family for living out of wedlock with her partner. I reflect on the harshness of this in today's enlightened times, but am comforted by the fact that at least she is making her own decisions about what is right for her, despite the pressure being put on her to conform to the strict values that she was brought up with.

She leaves with some determination to live her life according to her own value system, and, later, I hear with great pleasure that she has married her long term partner and is finally happy and at peace with herself and her life. No one deserved it more than her.

CHAPTER II
Nina's story

I had first taken Nina through a regression some ten years previously. She and her sister were part of a circle of friends that had been meeting to explore spiritual issues and she was also a participant in the Christos group regression. This particular technique was taken from Glaskin's early regression work in the 1970's.

A group experience, it requires at least four people to participate; one to massage the feet of the person being regressed, one to massage the third eye to stimulate the pineal gland and one to 'run' the regression for the subject. The combination of these different elements also serves to encourage a feeling of dissociation in the subject's mind, as there is just too much going on at the same time for the mind to process. A series of 'stretching' exercises follow, in which the subject is asked to visualise themselves growing longer, first through their feet and then through their head.

Nina's experience was one of the most powerful regressions that I have ever witnessed; perhaps even more so given that English was her second language. She had come to me wanting to explore why she was so terrified of driving. A mature woman, she had held her license for some time but was unable to get behind the wheel even to practice, without feeling overwhelmed by terror. With two children of school age, it had placed severe limitations on her life. As part of the preparation for the regression, I had taken her through the visual stretching exercises following the massaging of her feet and third eye which had been done by other group members. This left me free to concentrate on facilitating the regression process.

Here is her story, in her own words, related some ten years later just prior to her second regression. The past tense reflects the fact that she is remembering these details from back then, although, as she commented, the experience is as vivid today as it was back then.

"In the first one, (regression) I was a girl about 5 or 6 years old. I assume that the place could be Ireland or Scotland from the green pastures and the high cliffs. I was dressed in a brown tunic-like dress, my hair was curly and red and I was quite dirty. I opened a door of my house…it was a heavy wooden door and the house was made up of stones. When I opened the door, I saw a room with a thick wooden table. The smell of alcohol was very strong and there were my parents, they were fighting, yelling at each other. They didn't love me; they wanted a boy, not a girl. I was useless for them, just a problem…they didn't even notice me. I went out again and I ran with a boy of about my age with blond, reddish hair-he was my only friend. We ran through a very green field to the edge of a cliff and we sat there and watched the sea."

Next scene-I was driving an old van-it was in Canada and everything was covered in snow. I have two kids, a boy and a girl of about 3 and 4 years old, they had blond hair. I was very young myself too…early 20's. The kids were noisy, we were laughing…we started to sing a children's song. Suddenly, a deer crossed the road…I tried to avoid it…I crushed into a tree-I died! I crushed my chest into the steering wheel. My kids were alive, one unconscious, the other crying with blood on his face. I see my body lifeless, my spirit was desperate! They need help but none was around…and you know the rest. I felt terrible cold, although I was covered with a blanket and had an electric heater close to me, (we covered her with blankets when she started to shiver but she wasn't able to stop until after she came out of the regression) *When I opened my eyes, was like if I still was in another dimension-it took me a few minutes to organise my senses again."*

I remember instructing her to release the cellular memory of this experience-telling her it was ok to let it go now, knowing that it was not her fault, there was nothing she could have done to save them-it was just a terrible accident. We were all very moved by the experience and spent time reassuring her and soothing her. What happened afterwards was even more startling. Her story continues, still in her own words.

"After this regression I was able to drive, what for me was an impossible task. Even when I was 18 years old (you know how desperate teenagers are to drive!) I didn't grab the chance, although X who is now my husband tried hard to convince me. Surprisingly, I had not had major problems learning but it was a punishment for me. My vision become blurred, I had stomach cramps, as soon as I grab the steering wheel. In Argentina I was twice ready to get my license, but I didn't follow through.

Here in Australia, funny enough, when I went for the written test, I failed just one question. The lady told me "Oh God, is just one question (more) that you have wrong." She felt really sorry and suggested that I read the booklet once more and do it again. I was relief (sic) that I didn't get it right." (The unconscious will always find a way to protect us from what we most fear, usually through some form of subtle sabotage as in this instance.)

Months passed by and I tried again and I got my learning permission, but took me almost a year to call a driving instructor to take lessons. Finally, when I got my license I refused to drive. After the regression, gradually (but in a short period of time), I was able to drive!"

She had been able to change the message in her unconscious through releasing the emotional memories of the accident-she was free at last! Some ten years later, she is still driving and this is when she contacted me for another regression.

Her second one took place under different conditions. We did not have other group members to assist to recreate the Christos group experience and I decided to regress her using the standard hypnosis procedure that I had learned during my professional training with Brian in America.

She had come with issues relating to her husband and was keen to identify any previous lifetimes with him in the hope of establishing the lessons that they were meant to be learning from each other. We began by going back to her childhood.

"It's night time. Dad is sitting with me on the front door of our house; he's talking about the stars, telling me the names of them. Mum's there; it is a very hot summer night…we are eating ice cream…it's been a hot day and now it's a hot night. Love (smiling)…they love me.

I just make the connection that, in this present life, I always feel protected, loved, secure and accepted by my parents… very different than in other lifetimes," she notes. She is smiling and I leave her there to enjoy the memory for a while before regressing her back to just before her birth.

"Feeling trapped, uncomfortable…pressure, pushing…head hurts. I can't breathe." Her body is trying to move.

"Move your body as you need to," I encourage her.

"I'm moving now, can move. She wriggles as if going through the birth process. "Sticky!" (She wipes something away from her face, perhaps birth fluids.)

I check with her. "You are born now?"

"Yes." She is still. I leave her to rest for a while before instructing her to go back further until she finds a door that she needs to go through, trusting that her unconscious will know where to take her.

"Flying feeling, "she says suddenly. "Pleasant. Can't see anything." Afterwards, she told me that, at this point, she couldn't see a door; in fact she couldn't actually see anything at all. It was like a blank screen in front of her, and after a while she felt like she was falling down a tunnel or a tube.

"Just allow the images to appear when they will, trust whatever comes."

"Mountain…man on a horse passing by-hate him! (said with feeling) He's one of the landowners-he controls the villagers. I'm looking at him, he doesn't care-we are nothing to him! The people had no food, they all hate him. I am picking up a rock…feel so angry, then see myself running away, hiding. His men are searching for me…they grab me and bring me back. He can't control me anymore…she dies?" She is unsure, seeing flashes of information only, and fills in the gaps based on what her intuition tells her. The scene changes. "I'm the wife of a powerful man…at a party with others. People come to me, everyone listens to me. I know that people don't love me…I don't treat them with respect, don't care about them, only me. I had a baby but I abandoned him, he didn't fit in with my plans…wanted to be with the powerful man." She is quiet for a while as her unconscious searches for more information, then exclaims suddenly.

"The baby was my husband now. I abandoned him, just left him!" She is horrified at the callousness of her actions. "I'm dying-they poisoned me. I'm angry…it's not good. Her body movements reflect her agonising death and I remind her that she can detach and float above the scene if she wishes."

"What is the lesson you were meant to learn from this experience?"

"Compassion…for the people around me…for him. He was the baby I abandoned!' she realises. "I didn't care about him, he didn't serve my purpose. I was looking for another man-Pedro. I was a rich woman hiding my pain; I left my baby for a position of power."

"Who is the man you married? Look into his eyes," I instruct her.

"My old friend Heather." She smiles.

I summarise her insights with her afterwards.

"In this lifetime it seems that you feel angry at your husband because of his need and dependency on you, yet because of his bad childhood experiences, you feel compelled to mother him-perhaps to compensate for not mothering him before in the previous life. That karmic debt is paid now, you don't need to mother him anymore," I tell her. *"It is not your responsibility to compensate for his bad childhood in this lifetime or the previous one. You can have a different type of relationship with him as two equal adults, or you can leave. You are free to choose. If he tries to make you responsible, you can just tell him that you know he will find the answers himself and that you have complete faith in him to do that. That is the biggest compliment we can pay someone, to let them know that we believe in them and their ability to resolve their own problems. The lesson is one of compassion, for yourself as well as others. You are not being controlled, you choose your behaviour. Let go and trust."*

When I follow her up later, she is able to give me valuable feedback about the comparison between both regression experiences.

"I found the first one, the one that we did years ago, more powerful. Both were very good, but being such a left brained person, the strong emotions that I felt, for me were without any doubt a confirmation that what I saw was real and not my imagination. I clearly remember that with the first ones, when the first imagines (sic) were starting to come up, I thought –are you imagining this? But the emotions were so powerful that (they) override any thoughts. This time, was very difficult to see, were like fragments, and the feelings were not so strong. I just told you this as feedback, however, saying that, may also be a problem of my own expectations or resistance on my part."

This feedback was very important for me as it taught me not to make assumptions about how an individual is likely to experience a regression based on past experience. Each time is different, and it is vitally important to watch for the visual cues to identify what is happening for the person and adjust what you are doing accordingly. I hear later from her sister that she has left her marriage, unable to create the change that she wanted. Finally, she feels free of the weight of responsibility, having understood the karmic lesson.

PERSONAL NOTES

The gateway

SECTION 4

HEALING TRAUMA AND PHOBIAS

CHAPTER 12
Donna's story

Donna had been recommended for regression work by her chiropractor who knew of the work that I was doing. She had been treated for some time for a pronounced limp and when she walked, I noted that her body collapsed heavily onto her right side as though her left side was unable to bear any weight. She also admitted to suffering bouts of depression and was unable to experience much joy in her life, choosing instead to devote herself to her work and her teenage son and his needs. Now divorced, she knew that this mutual dependency was not good for him or herself. She wanted both of them to grow, but was terrified to let him go. During our initial discussion, Donna told me that she had been in a severe car accident when she was younger in which her boyfriend was killed. She did not remember much about the accident but had experienced problems with her leg since then. Understandably, she was nervous about regression work, fearing that it would take her somewhere she did not want to go. I explained that the process was entirely under her control and that we could stop at any time if she became uncomfortable. Where she went, would be up to her unconscious to decide.

Surprisingly quickly, she is able to access an early memory of problems with her back.
"I'm on the farm," she tells me, "horse…I'm jumping…black-he's difficult! If he trips I fall, hurt my back." She winces, "I fell on my back…it's painful. I'm waiting for someone to help me…mum comes and tells me off…it's very painful. I've done wrong again," she says unhappily.
"What stands out the most from this experience?" I wonder.
"Hoping to prove I was doing really well…didn't get the praise I was hoping for." Like many others of that era, she was raised by stern parents who still carried the vestiges of an earlier Victorian attitude towards raising children. We go to an earlier memory.

"Younger…quite...small. I'm on a horse with someone. It's wet and windy, horse jumped to the side and I fell into a puddle of water. I'm quite shocked…a lady helps me back on." I wonder about her fascination with horses. "It's exciting," she tells me. As she seems quite relaxed, I tell her to go to the source of her current problems, deliberately keeping it vague so that her unconscious can make the decision.
"Coldness…still. Someone is screaming…think it's an accident."
Immediately, sensing that she has gone to the one place she did not want to go, I cover her with a warm blanket and remind her that she can stop or float above the scene and come back whenever she wants to. She nods in acknowledgement and then frowning, continues. "Confusion…not sure what is happening."
"What is happening in your body?"
"I'm looking down more…it's me…crumpled." I am relieved for her sake that she is able to detach and view it from a distance. "Front seat's empty…talking…more confusion… man…he's standing outside, looking in. Don't know him." She frowns and continues, "can see cardigan I was wearing…" Gently, I encourage her and reassure her that she is safe now. "Yes," she acknowledges, and then moves restlessly.

"Front seat's empty, no one there." She sounds surprised. "Can see steering wheel…brown upholstery…seats…keep thinking, where's the driver? He's gone, not there to help." She sounds panicked as well she would be and I question her gently.

"Is anyone else there with you?"

"A lady and a man…the driver's run away." She is piecing the terrible scene together now. "Man…blue uniform…my chest feels heavy…don't want to look beside me." My eyes fill with tears for her, at the ghastly situation she finds herself in, and sensing her panic at the thought of what or who is beside her, I quickly remind her.

"You don't have to look."

Again the nod, her conscious mind has registered that she has a choice. "I try to keep my attention on them…feel like I know what's happening…I don't want to," she affirms. "They are stopping me from seeing anything else, they are talking to me, I keep my attention on them, know what is happening…my boyfriend's there…he's not moving…not making any noise. They are trying to keep my focus on other things. I can accept the reality of it now." I marvel at the way the unconscious lets her have the understanding a little at a time, so that she can deal with it. She sounds detached but aware; much healing can come from this and I leave her with the silence so that she can process it in her own way.

"I need to say goodbye," she says suddenly.

"You can do it in your own way," I remind her, suddenly afraid that she will be tempted to turn and look beside her. This is not an image that I want her to be left with, however, I trust that her conscious mind will protect her and will not allow her unconscious to reveal anything that she is unable to cope with.

She takes her time and at a nod from her, I take her back to the garden where her body has been resting, refreshing and healing during this experience.

"You can ask your guides and helpers about the lessons that you are meant to learn from this experience," I remind her.

"I'm to be grateful for the experiences I have had and for what I have learned," she tells me. While I am trying to make sense of this, she adds, "I must be glad…grateful for what I have come out with…my family, my life…" Now I understand, she has been given the gift of life to enjoy and this experience has helped her to see this. There is joy in her face.

"The aching sadness has gone," She is smiling now. "The driver did run away," she tells me afterwards. "He just went and left us to die," she says sadly and we reflect together on the terrible price he would have had to pay for this decision.

The relief she feels at having this memory made conscious is palpable. It is over, and finally she can leave it in the past where it belongs as part of her life experience. Some weeks later, I follow her up to see how she is. She is the happiest she has ever been, she tells me. Although she still has her limp, her body is lighter, easier and, when she is ready, she will come back for more healing. Interestingly, she tells me that at one time in her early twenties, after the accident and during a more confident stage in her life, her limp almost disappeared for a while. I know then that there is more we can do and reassure her that there is no rush; she can leave it until she is ready. Later she wrote to me and I have reproduced part of her letter below to show how much healing can come from trauma being released from the body.

My regression therapy with Valarie has allowed me to finally put to rest the sadness and grief I have held for 35 years. I have since made enormous changes in my life. I am now happy and relaxed and am able to speak about my accident and the loss of my loved one without the overwhelming emotions I once felt. My life has changed considerably, and I am forever grateful to Valarie.

On a cautionary note, I would like to add here that I do not believe that regression or trauma work should be undertaken by someone other than a professionally trained counsellor or psychologist. It is at best unhelpful, and in the worst case scenario, potentially dangerous to take someone to such a place and then leave them to deal with the aftermath of the experience without professional support and guidance. Just remembering something painful, is not in itself enough to heal it, and we need to remember that not everyone has the emotional resilience to be able to deal with these kinds of experiences. This is also why it is so important to assess the individual's suitability for this kind of work before proceeding. For these reasons, I will not do regression work with someone who is suffering from severe depression or who has significant mental health issues, although it is sometimes possible to work with them in other ways with a view to later regression work if not contra indicated. This is an important point that Brian Weiss reinforced in his professional training.

CHAPTER 13
Fiona's story

Phobias are often the end result of several fearful experiences which have been laid down over a long period of time, one layered over another with a resultant increase in fear each time. Often, the initial cause of the phobia is hidden because of this 'layering' of experience which increases the anxiety exponentially, leading to a particular event or trigger to which the phobia becomes attached.

One client sought help as a result of a life long phobia of storms. Married with teenage children, he was crippled by his fear of being caught outside in bad weather. His life was spent in an exhausting daily check of weather conditions and many times family outings had to be cancelled because of approaching rain. Desperate for some relief, he had opted to try hypnotherapy.

The sessions were excruciatingly painful for him. He was terrified of having to relive his experiences and only agreed to regression after several sessions of counselling and a relaxation trial. His first experience took him to a time in his childhood when he became lost in the bush after being out with his mates who had left him behind. His anxiety was extreme and was to be the start of an escalating fear which surfaced whenever he was in an anxiety provoking situation. Like many men of his age, he had suppressed his emotions believing any display of fear to be weakness which only served to increase his anxiety. Although his fear subsided sufficiently to enable him to drive in stormy weather, he was unable to attend long enough to work through the various layers that had been laid down over such a long period of time. I felt sad for him that we had been unable to clear the emotional charge sufficiently to enable him to have the peace and contentment that he deserved in his life.

In contrast, Fiona came seeking help with managing her breathing during her regular meditation practice. A relatively simple issue on the surface, her regression was to reveal a much deeper problem. She believed that her shallow breathing prevented her from going as deep as she would like to. During the intake session, she also mentioned a profound fear of going in the water which held her back considerably in her family life. Suspecting a connection between her fear and the shallow breathing, I recommended a regression and she agreed although she was nervous about what might come up. Initially, she had some trouble selecting a happy memory from childhood and I suspected that her conscious mind was still editing and controlling the process, which indicated that she was still finding it difficult to relax. I decided to make the instruction more specific in the hope that this would help, and asked her to go to her earliest happy memory.

Immediately, the memory came. "Birth of my daughter…caesarean…theatre-I'm apprehensive," she tells me. Then, "feel a tugging sensation …I'm afraid, but my husband is with me. Bright lights…my daughter is born-she's beautiful!" She is smiling with happiness and I leave her there for a while to relax a little more and enjoy the memory. Her next memory takes her back to early childhood.
"In Nanna and Papa's garden. Miss you." The tears trickle softly down her face as she remembers and I know then that she is entering a deeper state. "Felt safe then, open space…looking out on park…can see washing line. I'm making

tent out of sheets with my brother." She smiles at the memory and adds, "about ten years old…remember Nanna's pancakes…their love." The tears trickle softly down her face.

I ask her to go to the source of the problems in her current life, but at this point the fear takes over and I move quickly to reassure her.

"Remember back to the birth of your daughter when you were afraid. You knew there would be a beautiful outcome at the end of it and you had the support of your husband there. You were safe and that gave you the strength to go forward. On the other side of this experience will be a good outcome, to be able to move forward in your life, to enjoy it. You are safe here, in my office, and I am here to support you now."

She sighs as if releasing something and immediately goes to a past life memory.

"Feel a heavy weight pressing on my chest…can't breathe. I'm on a ship…old ship…wooden boards…sixteenth century…like the Cutty Sark. There's a storm…ship's breaking up! Can't move my legs and arms-I'm trapped!" Her terror is reflected in her face.

"You can detach and float above the scene, I remind her. View it from a distance."

"Everyone's panicking," she continues more calmly. Her head is moving restlessly from left to right. "its mayhem…fire…I'm calling for help…why is no one coming?" She is terrified and I remind her quickly of where she is.

"You are quite safe now, you are in my office and I am with you to help you, do you understand?"

She nods "yes" and continues. "There's no one to help me," she confirms, resigned now. There is a period of silence and, as she seems calm, I leave her there to process it in her own way.

"I can see lights," she tells me suddenly.

"Are you passed over?"

"Yes." She is calm and peaceful, in a place of serenity and I instruct her to access any messages that her guides and helpers may have for her about this experience and leave her to come back when she is ready.

Some clients process much of their information in the quiet state and so it is with Fiona. Afterwards she told me that just prior to the past life regression, she heard the message, "Remember the drowning," and after the regression, "Believe in yourself." With this information, Fiona was able to identify other issues of perfectionism and self criticism which were impacting upon her life. Her spiritual guidance provided the answers during her quiet, reflective period. "Let go and enjoy life, be spontaneous with your work focus and others," they say to her. "Find the child part."

Afterwards, she tells me that she loves photography but tends to get caught up in trying to get each shot as perfect as possible, which detracts from her enjoyment of the whole process. We spend some time discussing how it could be beneficial to bring some of the child's spontaneity into the process. Later I followed her up to see how she was doing and received the following message.

"I'm doing well. I've been on a meditation retreat and do a weekly meditation class and feel I'm going deeper, so the regression helped. I also venture into the sea-up to my armpits which was a first, so all in all, I felt it helped."

I am pleased for her that now she can enjoy water activities with her children, remembering that her fear prevented her from even going into their swimming pool with them before.

CHAPTER 14
Mandy's story

In contrast, Mandy's story was all the more intriguing because she had not come with any specific purpose in mind. A member of our women's circle which met fortnightly to share experiences and further spiritual development, she was curious about the regression process. A quiet and insightful woman, we always looked forward to her presentations. She had expressed an interest in having a regression, more as a step on her spiritual journey than to resolve any particular problem. As she was a little anxious, I spent a considerable time on the relaxation process, wanting her to be quite comfortable before I began regressing her.

After a while, her breathing became deeper and her skin tone began to change, both indicators that the person is entering a state of deep relaxation. As Mandy had no particular issue that she wanted to explore, I took her straight to her childhood and asked her to indicate when she found a memory that she wanted to explore. Soon I got a small nod 'yes' and, as I had instructed her earlier in the relaxation, she was able to talk and yet remain in a deep state.
She began hesitantly. "It's my birthday party, I'm four years old ….there are four people that I know…Angela, my best friend… one with blonde hair…..my mum's there. We're in the front room of the house. (she pauses, her eyelids flickering, so I know she is seeing the scene) It's filled with sunshine…there's a table in the middle of the room, four chairs around it…sideboard…birdcage on an old fashioned stand. I can see my mother…I'm happy…overwhelmed"
She stays with the memory for a while and as she is smiling, I leave her to enjoy it before regressing her further.
"Its earlier…I shared a room with my brothers," she offers eventually. "I'm going to bed…waiting for grandfather to say goodnight. Its fun, even though he's stern…we muck around after he's gone. My brothers shared a double bed…I had a single bed by the side." She pauses as if she is thinking. (This change from past to present language is characteristic of a regression and indicates the person's ability to move between past and present states simultaneously) "It must have been winter as in summer we slept in the attic." Her conscious mind provides the explanation. I wait and as there seems no more to come from this memory, move her back further in time.
"I see me as a baby…I'm six or seven months, sitting in an old fashioned pram in a fish and chip shop. My grandparents owned it…mum used to work there (pauses) I can picture a bonnet…not sure…can see the edge of it. I can see the counter…windows behind me."
Wanting to establish her state, I ask her "are you happy?"
"Yes. I'm wearing a dress…I've got a chip in my hand." She says all this in a matter of fact tone, as though it is usual for her to be there. She seems quite content and we remain here for a while before I decide to try regressing her to an earlier time.

I ask her to imagine becoming lighter and floating up into the clouds. This is a good way to break the connection with the childhood memories and set the scene for another time, although I never ask the person to go to a past life, preferring it to be their choice. I bring her gently down to earth and ask her to describe what she sees.
"Swampy ground…marshes…rushes." I ask her what she is wearing on her feet to try and establish a time. "Nothing!" she exclaims in surprise and continues on. "I'm wearing a skirt…brown…a top, pale blue and I have blond hair. There's a river or pond in front of me…I'm standing on the bank." I ask her how she's feeling. "I'm happy," she replies simply and goes on to explain to me, "I work on a farm." She pauses, her eyelids flickering again. "I can see a castle …there's a

forest behind me." There is a long pause and I ask her if she would like to go there, trying to gauge whether to try and move her on. "I don't want to go to the castle," she says firmly. "Who lives there?" I ask her curiously. "Landowners," she replies dismissively and I get the impression from her tone that she doesn't like or approve of them. She continues, "someone's there, on a horse…he's leaning down to talk to me… dark haired…brown leather clothes…his horse is brown too. I don't feel afraid. Don't think I know him." (this in answer to my question, I'm trying to establish if this is someone from her current lifetime that she knows) "He's riding away." I ask her the purpose of the conversation. "Just to talk, like a flirtation," she explains, "it wouldn't go anywhere." I wonder if this man is to do with the castle, perhaps of a higher status than her and wait for her to continue. "I'm going back to the forest now," she continues. "I see a cottage…thatched roof, smoke coming from the roof."

"Who lives here? I prompt her. "I do. I see a woman…think there's a man. It's pretty but dark inside…just one room with beds partitioned off…curtains…animals, chickens, pigs. I'm happy with my life." I instruct her to let the story unfold like a movie and tell me what happens to her in this life.

"I think I do die," she says sadly. "I'm strangled by someone from the castle… a knight…black garment…I see hands coming for my neck," she struggles, seeming upset. I ask her why she thinks this is happening, hoping to establish the reason for this memory.

"Because he can," she says simply and continues; "I can't breathe!" Her hand goes to her throat as if in distress and I ask her what her last thoughts are as she dies, instructing her to float above the scene to put an end to her pain. "I'll miss my parents," she says sadly, "I'm still young." I take her back to the garden, her peaceful scene from the induction, and suggest that she allow her guides, helpers or some wise person to come to her and help her with the lesson that she is meant to learn from this experience. (There always seems to be some kind of link with the experiences from a person's current lifetime)

She speaks as if repeating what she hears. "Child, you are not to blame, let it go." There seems nothing more and so we finish there and I bring her back.

Over a hot drink, we discuss the experience and I ask her what she thinks of the message and whether she feels that she does hang on to self blame or guilt. She nods in agreement and I ask her whether she has any particular physical problems in her body. "Yes, I can't wear anything tight around my neck," she tells me. "In fact, if Mark goes to touch me there, (she demonstrates how her teenager makes a playful grab for her throat) I can't bear it!" She flinches at the memory and then her eyes open wide in surprise as she connects the experience of being strangled with the problem with her neck. I explain that often physical problems in this current lifetime appear directly connected to the manner of death in a previous lifetime. In many cases, the problem disappears after a regression as the cellular memory is released by the re-experiencing and subsequent letting go of the emotion surrounding the event.

Some time after the regression, I asked Mandy about the uncomfortable feeling around her neck and she reported that it had eased considerably. It is possible that there were other past life injuries connected with her neck and that further regression work may help to clear this problem altogether for her.

PERSONAL NOTES

Transformation

SECTION 5

PHYSICAL HEALING

CHAPTER 15
Mary's story

The physical healing that comes from regression work is one of the most satisfying aspects of the work. To be able to assist someone in releasing long held trauma from the body and witnessing their joy at living a life free of the old pain is truly rewarding.

Roger Woolger's extensively researched book 'Other Lives, Other Selves,' discusses the pioneering work done by Morris Netherton who proposed a strong link between past life memories and physical complaints in this life. He concluded that a surprising number of physical complaints do have a past life story behind them which, when re enacted cathartically, led to rapid recovery and relief of painful symptoms. My experiences with clients also confirmed this. Here are some of their stories.

Mary approached me for a regression to help her identify the cause of a long standing physical complaint. She had been suffering from uncomfortable abdominal pressure and pain in her urethra with frequent urges to urinate for about eight years. Understandably, this was severely impacting her quality of life; she was nervous about leaving her home in case she needed to urinate and was becoming increasingly isolated. Medical check ups had not been able to find any discernible physical cause. On an emotional level, she had not experienced happiness in her relationships with men. During the conversation, she mentioned the 'low blow' she had felt in connection with a recent experience that she viewed as a betrayal. As her hands went instinctively to her abdomen, I immediately began to suspect an underlying emotional cause.

Mary was Nina's sister and had also been part of the Christos group regression experience some ten years before. They were very close and her sister had requested that she be present during her recent regression. Interestingly enough, during her sister's regression, Mary also experienced a sharp pain in her abdomen and she suspected a link to her sister's experience with her husband. Both women had found the group experience to be very vivid and powerful and she was eager to have a regression herself to try and identify, and hopefully clear, the source of her painful symptom. The problem was going to be how to re-create the depth of the Christos experience without the assistance of other people to help with the massaging.

I decided to massage her feet during the relaxation induction and ask her to hold the feeling of the sensation there as I massaged her third eye. She was soon relaxed and was able to accomplish the visual stretching exercises very easily, being familiar with the procedure.

Next, I instructed her to imagine her body becoming lighter and lighter and to allow herself to begin to float, like a giant balloon, upwards into the air, before coming down to rest outside her front door which she was to describe. Almost immediately, she began to talk, obviously in a very deep state as evidenced by the flickering of her eyelids and the quietness of her voice - I had to strain to hear her.

"Can see the carport…bushes…roof tiles." She is smiling. "My legs are so long! Wide at the top and narrow at the bottom…my feet are huge!" (This is a common visual distortion that often occurs as a result of the visual stretching exercises) "I can see a big spider web…have to get it." There is quiet while she 'cleans it up' and then she frowns suddenly and I know something else is happening.

"What are you experiencing?"

"Cold breeze…coming through my crown chakra," she murmurs, "feel different …connected with something… like receiving a current…" She seems puzzled and adds helpfully, "its dark…I'm separated from my body…behind it somehow…I feel sad." There is a silence, then "I want to go away from there," she says suddenly, "feel that pressure…." She winces, clearly uncomfortable.

"You can do that," I tell her. *"You can go to the source of the pressure and pain in your current lifetime if you wish."*

I want to give her the option, knowing that her unconscious will take her where she most needs to be.

"It's misty…dark…sensation…someone kicking me there." She holds her abdomen and frowning continues. "See man's boot…high boots…black…can see buckle…I'm poor, young, thin, long straight blond hair, parted in middle, old skirt, creamy colour, vest…brownish colour. I'm lying curled up on the floor." There is so much detail which tells me it is a very vivid experience for her and I ask her if she knows who the man is.

"No…can't see his face, just his boot coming at me. It's the turn of the century," she adds. "In the countryside somewhere…"

"Why is he kicking you?"

"He's upset with me…I'm working for him."

She continues to flinch and I suggest that she detach from the experience and view it from a distance but she is unable to do so and I decide to move her on to spare her any further distress.

"You can fast forward it like a movie." I tell her. *"What happens to her?"*

"I'm floating…" She lets her breath out in a long sigh, relieved. "Big blue disc in front of me…dark…peaceful… lights…" then, quickly, she is in pain again. "Pressure," she gasps, clutching her abdomen.

"Go to the source of the pain," I instruct her.

"Birth,' she gasps, "pulling…pushing sensation. It hurts…like contractions." She is distressed.

"Are you giving birth?" I ask.

"No…didn't want to have it…the abortion…" She cries and I feel for her, unwilling to intervene, knowing this will ultimately be healing for her, to release the cellular memory. She feels the urgent need to urinate and I bring her out and assist her to the bathroom. When she returns, I check with her that it is ok to take her back in so that we can do some healing. It is a measure of her trust in me that she agrees. She has pain in her left foot so I decide to try moving the pain down through her foot and out of her body and instruct her accordingly. She becomes more relaxed as she does this and then connects with her guides and helpers to establish the lessons behind her experiences and to assist in her healing. Previously, she thought of herself as 'just a convenience' and 'not belonging.' Now she is willing to consider the possibility of having a healthy relationship with someone honest, generous and caring who likes to share. For perhaps the first time, she is able to believe that she will meet someone who respects her and values her for who she is. There is no need for her to punish herself anymore.

Later, I followed up with her to see how she was and she told me that she had been experiencing intense sadness; however, she knew that she was mourning the loss of her child and was finally able to allow herself the grief that she had suppressed for so many years. Here is her account in her own words;

During the session I experienced intense pain (as experienced during the worst time of this process). The session needed to be interrupted several times (to allow her to go to the toilet).

It wasn't until after the session and because of what came out during the regression that I was able to associate the intense pain during urination and the sudden and painful spasms with labour pains. It also came to my mind what the doctor said to me after the completed procedure (abortion). "I've never had anyone who resisted so much." (NB How sad that he did not explore this with her at the time instead of just proceeding) During the next couple of days after having the regression, I felt sad. I was still grieving the loss of that 'boy' and I was able somehow to feel his energy close to my body (upper body, left shoulder). Gradually, the sadness lifted and I felt freer, lighter. It is worth to mention that not long after Val's session, the pain completely disappeared.

She also said that she felt secure during the session, safe. "I wasn't sure whether I was imagining or actually reliving the experience," she noted, "not until I was amazed with the outcome. It was not in my consciousness.

Later, she returned, eager to have another regression to see if she could heal the bowel irritation which she felt was also connected, and we arranged to meet the following week. I was pleased for her that this first, intense experience had led to some physical healing for her. Quickly, comfortable with the process now (I can't stress enough how important this is, to have some prior interaction and knowledge before the regression), she entered a trance state as evidenced by her long, slow breaths. She was an experienced meditator and it showed.
"I'm incontinent…in my 80's she tells me. "Can see the back of myself, short, white straight hair, chubby. I'm ashamed…no one around me…old house, isolated…country area. Am in a big wooden room…big wooden beam across one of the walls…sitting by myself…very unsafe. Can't move, sitting down, holding on in my bum, can't go to the toilet, can't walk." She is deeply upset. "I'm facing the door but can't do anything by myself. There's no noise, nothing, precarious place!" I sense her fear and distress and remind her that she is able to detach from her body and float above the scene if she wishes.
"They left me, they left me behind," she cries. Tears are slipping from her eyes and I encourage her to let them go, knowing that more healing will come from their release.
"What happens to you?" I ask her after a period of silence.
"Blue light…I'm not there any more. I don't have any body experience," she explains, then corrects herself. "I'm aware of my rectum…peaceful…I don't know where I am…don't think I am dead…no, I'm waiting to die." Her eyelids are flickering rapidly now. "No real pain…peaceful." She smiles then begins to fidget.
"Feel something on my right side…neck area…energy, not uncomfortable. I'm dying, feel my throat…tummy. Physical tunnel," she tells me, "throat…guts…feet." I sense that her conscious mind wants me to understand the process that she is going through; we are both energy workers in our respective fields.
"Funny sensation," she adds, "not painful…not comfortable either."
"What are your thoughts as you die?" I ask, wanting to capture the experience for her.
"Doesn't bother me," she says dismissively. The question is irrelevant to her; she is making sense of it in her own way. "Examination…procedure?" she muses aloud. "No one else is there…hospital…beds around me…don't see anyone either, just a knowledge," she explains. Suddenly a frown crosses her face and her eyebrows go up. "Trying to take something out of me…" The movement of her eyebrows is an indication of the discomfort attached to the procedure. "Internal exam…window at back of me…another bed in front of mine…bed to my left…large well lit room… operation?" Again she winces in discomfort. "They pull something out…tingling down my leg." I wonder if she is re experiencing the abortion and quickly remind her to disconnect and float above her body if she needs to.
"I'm in the country, not the city…Europe," she gasps. The recollections are coming fast and furious now with the releasing of the cellular memory. "I'm in pain now…down there." Her body movements indicate that she is clearly in distress and I ask her if she wants to come back.
"Need to go to the toilet, "she gasps. Her face is screwed up with pain and I gently assist her to get down from the table and make sure she is out of the experience and back in present time before assisting her to go and relieve herself. When she returns, I place her back into trance for some healing, knowing that her body needs to let go of the memory and

integrate the experience so that she can continue to heal. We do some energy release work and sit down afterwards to discuss the experience over a hot cup of tea.

"What lessons do you think you are meant to learn from this experience?" I ask her.
"To look after myself," she replies immediately. She knows.
"I felt a hand on my tummy," she tells me, and a voice saying, 'you are not looking after yourself. You must love yourself, put yourself first, make time for yourself.' She is nodding to herself, acknowledging the truth of these words, and we take some time to discuss how she will do that.
"Watch what I eat, not rush, make time for me," she says simply. She knows what to do and I leave her quietly reflecting, looking forward to her feedback.

Again, I hear later from her that the discomfort in her bowel has lessened considerably. At long last, her body is healing and her mind is free of the critical thoughts that tormented her previously. This gives me great pleasure, to know that I have been able to help her continue the wonderful energy healing that she does free of the pain that plagued her.

CHAPTER 16
Gloria's story

Gloria came to see me besieged with a variety of problems in her current life that were causing her much distress. She told me that she was not comfortable in her body from the legs down had deep fears around the areas of poverty and commitment. She had been referred by someone else and was eager to go straight into a regression experience.

We talked for a while so that I could assess her suitability for regression. Regression work is not advisable in cases where there is a severe mental health disorder, or if the individual has a very fragile ego, and I need to feel confident that this is likely to help rather than hinder the person before proceeding. I also spent some considerable time with the relaxation part as I had not seen her before, and establishing an atmosphere of trust is an important part of the process. Generally, I prefer to see someone a couple of times before doing a regression so that we can develop some kind of relationship before we begin, but that is not always possible.

Initially, her excitement appears to make it difficult for her to relax completely. I asked Gloria to try and let go of any particular expectations and tell her to 'just see where it goes' so that she can relax more easily and gain maximum benefit from the experience. She visibly relaxes and at my prompting, is able to go back to an earlier childhood experience.
"I'm dancing in the lounge, teaching my cousins to dance…playing. All dressed up. Got my stockings on - too big for them." She speaks in a staccato style, pausing briefly between phrases, seemingly eager to get the words out. "Teaching them to dance in front of stereo. Family having barbecue . Am wearing black leotard, yellow lycra stockings…12 years old…doing something I enjoyed. Happy experience. Enjoy teaching - something I was good at…family thought I was good at it," she adds on reflection.
We stay here a while longer but she begins to fidget and I take the cue and move her on, knowing that she is eager for a past life experience. However, as is often the case, her expectations get in the way of her being able to let go completely. (I do encourage people to come for an initial visit before the regression, to enable us to build rapport and deal with realistically with expectations which may get in the way, but sometimes time constraints or excitement can affect the process).

She moves her head restlessly from side to side. "My head feels blocked," she frowns, seemingly frustrated with herself. I soothe her and instruct her to go back to another childhood memory that has a bearing on her current difficulties. It does seem the case, as surmised by Dr Weiss, that someone will go to current life issues first for resolution before going back further to past lives.
She begins again. "Going to visit father in school holidays - locked in his room while he sleeps. Frustration, waiting …hated afternoon sleeps. I am 4 years old, have blonde hair, almond shaped eyes - I look like my son! "she realises with some surprise. "I am just waiting - want him (father) to be awake - I am bored." I note that she was also showing impatience here too at a young age, wanting to move on from where she is, and wonder if patience might be the over riding issue. However, I keep my thoughts to myself, not wanting to influence her in any way.
She continues. "In pram - being pushed around by my mum. We are looking for my father, eating Chinese food in the pram. Sense mum's frustration, confused about being in the pram. Mum's upset…having big sighs…anger. I am watching her face - can tell how she's feeling. I feel sad too, but there's nothing I can do, I'm too little."(Often this

happens with those who regress to babyhood, they have an instinctive knowledge of what is happening for the parent, usually the mother, with whom there is an intense physical bond).

Suddenly she jerks and goes straight into another experience, taking me by surprise. "Feeling in legs - heavy…pulled down…numb…pressure on my coccyx….push down on it," she tells me quickly, apparently wanting me to know where she is. "Am lying on my stomach, can't move legs. Am lying on a big wooden slab, big bolts in it…someone's pushing down." She frowns again. "It's like it is a bit of relief. Someone's trying to work on me, pushing down on my sacrum. I am a female, big skirt on, one of the kitchen maids. I see a smooth wooden table. I work there; in the kitchen…see a big fire. Like in Oliver Twist days," she explains. "Pain…period…relieves it….like deep tissue massage. My legs feel heavy - no feeling."

"What is wrong with you?" I ask, trying to ascertain why she can't move.

"I am just stuck there on the table…I'm not upset," she adds quickly.

"What do you tell yourself about this?" I ask her, wanting her to tell me what the connection is.

"It's just the way I am. Feels like a doctor working on me…he's wearing a hat…big squarish hat…big red cheeks…older man, jovial."

" What does he tell you?"

"This will be good for you." He is like a cartoon character almost. The room is like a kitchen…pots and pans…open fire. My pain is relieved."

"How did you get the pain?" I ask her curiously.

"Spinal defect - that's the way I am. Feel like a servant…kitchen cook…feel comfortable there. In England somewhere….grimy, dirty, like out of Oliver Twist movies. Sound like one of those girls from Oliver Twist…Quiet. I die young, feel useless, so poor and crippled." She is quiet and there seems to be no more, so I take her back to the garden in her relaxation and instruct her to ask her guides the meaning of this lifetime.

She is quiet for some time, nodding as though hearing someone speak to her, and signals when she is ready to return as we had agreed.

"The lesson is to have an understanding of what being in pain is like," she explains, sitting up quickly in excitement. "Do back massages, spinal work. Feel what they are feeling. Understand what feeling stuck in the legs is like - develop compassion. - understand what it feels like to be trapped." She pauses and smiles, "In this lifetime, I have no reason to feel like that- I'm holding myself back by handing responsibility over to others - maybe someone will come and save the day." She laughs at herself.

I nod in acknowledgement. "Do you have an understanding of what you must do now?" I ask her.

"Yes," she replies simply. "I have known for a little while. I'm feeling healthy in my body. I am free now- can do it on my own terms."

She tells me what she thinks the possible lessons are that she is meant to learn.

"Not entrapping myself- cloister myself in. I need to feel more confident outside, know that I am safe now." Her voice is strong, sure. She leaves happily and I sense that she will finally move into the massage work that she feels she is destined to do.

CHAPTER 17
Cheri's story

Cheri was an attractive woman in her late fifties who looked much younger. Interested in regression work after reading one of Brian Weiss's books, she was hoping to find an answer to the problem of her frequent desire to urinate which was, understandably, placing unwanted limitations on her life. She was also curious about why she and her husband had not had children in this lifetime.

Despite her misgivings, she was one of those fortunate individuals who could access the hypnotic state quite easily, and after a few minutes of encouragement, she was accessing a childhood memory.
"In my bed, brother was born. Father comes in to tell me that I had a baby brother. Sick and tired, I want to sleep. Surprised that he came in…came to school, made polony sandwiches for me because mum not there." She sounds pleased as she remembers this unaccustomed time with him. Her next experience explained his frequent absences.
"I'm on a plane…navy jet - sent for family. Leaving…going to Darwin. Wanted to get out but couldn't – trapped, sick…nauseous…not understanding what was going on. Not normal passenger plane…like a jet." Her father was a navy man and she tells me that the family were used to his frequent absences and the instability that it brought to their lives. I wonder if her problem originated from this early experience of being moved from a stable secure base, probably with very little warning, and decide to go back further in time to establish if there is any earlier origin to her anxiety. Initially, she has difficulty seeing anything, but has an overwhelming feeling of being stuck.

"Can't see anything-red everywhere, sky is red, smoky, red sky." She is very tearful at this point, there appears to be some strong emotion attached to this memory. "Can't see any people-there's nobody there! Can't find anybody…can't feel my body…can't see it…like in a mist…like a painting I have done. I can see a tepee – on the ground…want to look inside," but she is reluctant, seemingly afraid of what she might find.
"Is there anybody inside?" I ask her, wanting to encourage her to go in if she needs to.
"Can't see anyone…only left over fire…cold. Nobody is there," she tells me finally, "its empty. I am an Indian woman…tepee…like a high dwelling…primitive. Can't see surrounding countryside." I wait, curbing my impatience and she adds suddenly, "I can see to the left…rocks like ledges…flat…they're not round." She frowns as she struggles to make sense of what she is seeing. "They left me behind. Can't see myself, I'm not old, feel like a youngish woman, twenties."
"What happens to her?" I ask, wanting to progress her a little further.
"Have to leave tepee…," she tells me, "find out if anyone's left…have to leave shelter of rocks. Got skin dress on… raid?" She is questioning out loud, still trying to make sense of what she is seeing. "Don't feel injured…feel like I have been left behind…I'm scared. I don't know whether to go and look for them….go in another direction?" I wait for her to decide what to do, knowing that the next step must come from her.
"Have to go right-after them," she says decisively. "They have taken something of mine with them-can't let them take it…little boy…he's not Indian…he's got freckles. He's my little boy!" She is crying now, her grief is evident on her face. "Why are they taking him away? He's holding out his hand to me…he loves me…he wants me there! Someone is standing watching sternly…I have to explain myself…but I don't know what I have done wrong!" She is in agony.

"He looks like my younger brother…I'm very close to him. He's got my eyes! He's mine." There is a fresh outbreak of tears, before she manages to pull herself together.

"He's well," she reassures herself. "I have to go and leave him with this other woman." Then her emotions overwhelm her again, the pain of loss is excruciating. "I can't leave him! Why do I have to go? He's all right; he knows he has to go with this other woman. Why am I being made to leave?" She is conflicted between her love for him and her need to leave. "I don't feel ill…I have to do something else…have to look for someone…I have to go and find my husband." She is resolute now.

"I go to the left…search…there's a young man…important to me and my son. Villages…I might be in Scotland…deserted villages…coastal. I don't know if he wants me to look for him. He's gone to join up…fight? No, he wouldn't leave, he loves his son," she decides. "There are no people, I can't find him…I'm just sheltering now, despairing, so alone. I'm not part of anything. My little boy wants me to find him. I don't know if I want to find him." Then suddenly she exclaims, "I can see him! Oh, he's a fine man! He's got breast bands, gold red hair, blue eyes, spears. He's such a strong man…he's marvellous! God, he's so strong, he's a leader, he's wise, he knows everything." She seems in awe of him. "He sees me, he looks kind. He does want me, but "you know I have to do this thing," he tells me, "just come." We're together, but we have a job to do…sheltering other people. He's so damn fine! We will be together. I will help him. Want to leave it there," she says quickly. "I don't want to know what happens, don't want to spoil it…such a good memory."

Afterwards, she tells me that she was afraid of how it might end and just wanted to enjoy the encounter.

"Go to the source of the problem with your bladder," I instruct her, mindful that we have not yet identified a definitive source.

"It's annoying. I'm at kindy…I didn't make it (to the toilet)…black knickers…only one with them on the line drying, all the others are white." She is embarrassed, "I can't hold on…not speaking up." There is a silence and then; "Don't you dare!" I wonder who is reprimanding her. "I'm just a kid…woke up…can't find the door." At this point she cannot put off the urge any longer and we finish so that she can go to the toilet.

Cheri leaves, much taken with her experience and arranges to come back and 'finish the other half of the story,' as she puts it. What happens in the second session is to surprise both of us!

Again, she finds herself on a rocky ledge, only this time it is flat with lines in it, she tells me.

"Can see my feet…spatula like, different to now, thicker, browner…no sandals, barefoot," she says breathlessly, "can see my hands on the rocks…flat ones with ledges. I'm standing in a clearing, can't see much beyond." In answer to my question she replies, "don't feel anything, don't know why I'm here. Can see…like the Aztecs…flat rocks, like plateaux," then, in surprise, "there's villages in the hillsides! I can see a town down there." She is still puzzled by her situation. "I am high up, looking down, watching. I don't know what I am doing there." Finally she decides that she has to climb down there.

A hair raising ten minutes follows while she bumps and slips her way down the rocks. There are many 'ows' and exclamations as she collects scrapes and bruises on her way down. "I have to go over the edge," she tells me, "it's a huge risk, but I have to go. Finally, to both our great relief, she makes it to the other side.

"I'm rolling down," she tells me, "just have to get to the village to survive. There are buildings carved in rock. I'm a female or young man, bare legs, no boobs…must be a man. I'm down." Then, "I'm scared to go in, but I have to."

"Allow yourself to go where you need to go," I encourage her.

"I think I was undergoing some sort of test," she tells me, "but I didn't do it…have to go back and face them." She sees a man she recognises as her father and a woman grinding something into a pot. "He's disappointed in me…

my clothes are just about all ripped off. I didn't do what I was supposed to do…must go again. I have to go again!" There is real anguish in her voice, and suddenly I realise the implications of the words that she is saying and ask her to repeat them more slowly. "I have to go again, I have to go again." Finally, she makes the connection between these words and her frequent desire to urinate. As her unconscious brings the double meaning of the words to the attention of her conscious mind, she is incredulous and I explain to her how words can have more than one context. Often, these subliminal messages are the most powerful, sitting just below the level of ordinary waking consciousness; they can exert the most powerful effect on our behaviour. Bringing them into conscious awareness, as we have just done, allows her to release the power of the message "I have to go again," and replace it with something that will not trigger the urge to urinate.

She has one more glimpse of her future before we finish, and sees herself, older, content and looking out over the land again. "He's content," she affirms it to herself, "everything's a trial but you have to keep on going. I feel older, stronger. He's gone his way…not doing it the same as everyone else. He's achieved it his own way."
"Next time you find yourself with that urge to go," I tell her, "try saying, it's ok, I don't need to go. I have done it my way; I don't need to go again."

Two more lessons are revealed to her before we finish.
-The right path will reveal itself.
-My independence and my power are inner treasures.

Cheri left still somewhat bemused by the experience and determined to come back and finish the second half of her first story with the marvellous man – I was looking forward to it as much as her and several weeks later she returned from her holiday with good news. There were several days when she had experienced no problems at all; the constant desire to urinate just disappeared. However, it had not gone completely and we went into the next regression with this in mind.
"I'm crouching by a pool…underground?" she wonders out loud. "Primitive skin clothes on again…looking at myself crouching….waiting for someone. I'm frightened…can see my hands, nails a bit dirty….similar hands…wild looking hair…not brushed or combed. My sandals go across." She indicates with her hand where a strap crosses her foot. "I don't seem to be able to move …hiding?...waiting? Don't know what I'm waiting for." She frowns, "I'm pacing about a bit…on the edge of a ledge, its dark over the side, maybe a pool." She remains here hesitating for quite a while and I encourage her gently while refocusing her on her goal.
"Instruct your subconscious to take you where you need to go to resolve your current problem."
"Walking round a crevice in the rock…I'm going to go through…got to move it a bit…I'm getting through," she gasps. (It's obviously a tight fit!) "There's nothing on the other side!" She sounds disappointed. "I really want there to be something on the other side." Immediately, her subconscious picks up her instruction and she finds herself looking at a settlement of some sort.
"People are going about their chores. I don't know if they're setting something up or packing up…I must belong there," she muses. "They're looking at me…not hostile…," her eyelids are fluttering quickly as she scans the scene, then her head moves to the right. "I'm looking for something…through people's blankets, kicking them aside with my sandal…NO!" she exclaims suddenly and tears roll gently down her face as her mind assimilates what she is seeing.
"Whatever you experienced then will be released now," I reassure her gently.
"It's my little boy," she realises, "dead?...sleeping? He's got his thumb in his mouth." She frowns, trying to make sense of what she is seeing. "I don't know if he is alive or not, people are looking at me…I don't know what to do…I'm

holding onto him, he's not waking up…I think he's gone….peacefully gone…I want to resolve this," she cries in agony, "I've got to find out whether I did something wrong."

"Your tears are releasing the cellular memory," I remind her gently.

"There's a big man there," she says after a while. "Really don't know if he's my partner or the Chief. There's only a few of us, we are mostly wiped out…got to move somewhere else…like fugitives," she explains to me before returning to the little body. "I seem to want to pick him up and carry him. Yes we have to move on." She is still not sure if he is dead or not and decides to carry him on her back, maybe to bury him. "Moving through…very rocky…we are hiding…moving stealthily, coastal, bleak," she informs me. "There's only a few people left… primitive clothes, like skins, furs and things, not all rugged up. Fair skinned," she continues, "but grimy, not clean." She wonders aloud who they might be, this small band of persecuted people and comes to the conclusion that they might be Druids. "We are seeking safe ground," she tells me and then, "I need to know the purpose…what good we're doing," she says urgently. Immediately the answer comes to her. "We are like pilgrims…can see a Celtic cross…weapons there, donkeys, we don't look cold. Just wandering, looking for a place…frustrated, feels just like in my life now," she says, sounding despondent, "wondering what the purpose is." Her conscious mind seems to be analysing and bringing her back to the present, so I use a deepening technique to encourage the subconscious to take control.

"Now I'm dressed in a gown…Grecian…little band around my head…my little boy is smiling - he is alive!" she says excitedly. "Had to get him to a safe space… I must be someone important," she realises. "We're safe…big man that took us there is smiling…people are glad to see me and my little boy. They're all shouting and really pleased. It's really good," she smiles, happy at last with the outcome. Her summary says it all.

"We had a big journey and lots of obstacles, now we're safe…can move forward."

The importance of this realisation has implications for her current life too, and I feel sure that this is a metaphor chosen by her subconscious to enable her to move forward.   I leave her to make the next contact, knowing that she is now moving forward at her own pace.

CHAPTER 18
Annie's story

Annie had presented with a variety of health problems. She was the woman who died in a mudslide and was later able to identify both the incident and the little village where it occurred from her research on the internet. This time, she was anxious to investigate the cause of her itching navel which was 'driving her crazy,' she said, especially when she tried to go for a run. A health instructor, she was very committed to her fitness and this problem had been there for as long as she could remember. I decided to begin by taking her back to her birth to see if we could find any clues there before we investigated a past life.

Well used to the process, Annie was able to access a trance state very quickly.
"Baby, long umbilical cord…stars in space. Feel quite childlike. Colours, different colours swirling around. Giggling, I am part of a group of lights dashing around. There's a sense of urgency-got to go soon… 'Just one more time,' she pleads with them. "Now I'm 13, sliding down grass embankment on cardboard. In space, quite childlike – one more time before I have to go-don't want to go. Other home…sky, full of colours, pastel colours, got to go really quickly." She is an agony of indecision. "Just go!"she tells herself fiercely. "Still see baby there, naked, not being held. Can't understand why nobody's holding the baby." She is confused, going backwards and forwards between the sky and the baby's body. "I'm sensing distance between mother and me…not in the same room. I can see yellow, sun, green colour; I'm not in the baby's body." She finds herself looking down at the body, unwilling to enter it. The reason becomes apparent in her next words.
"Loneliness, my real friends are always up there, feel that love and support." She does not want to leave them, but she understands that she has to. "It's my turn to try it. You make the decision to come now," she tells herself firmly.

There is a period of silence. "Just gone through all my life," she tells me in amazement. "Began with hovering above baby…felt myself floating down. I'm just there, it's ok. It's as if the baby was purring," she tells me. "Focussed on umbilical cord…drying up and turning brown, falls off. Whizzing through my life, focussing on different stages, stalling on parts, seeing groups of different friends." She seems to be experiencing a life review very similar to that of a near death experience. Then, "I'm in snow now, five of us, group of us having a good time. Group of eighteen friends there. All the other times seem meaningless. Drawn to time when I had friends. Lady in my life at the moment, one of the original lights! Need to allow people in –reconnect with lights. All rushing into the circle, energies exploding like fireworks." Her face reflects the joy of reconnection and I leave her in the space for a while to enjoy it.

Finally, she is able to resolve the conflict within herself. She can accept that she made a decision to come into human form in this lifetime and the 'past life review' that she experienced enables her to finally accept this decision. The itching navel was merely an energetic imprint left from her attachment to the bardo state before this lifetime. She has no further problems with her navel and is able to resume her running free of the itching.

I decided to include Annie's story at the last minute because, as she says, it might help others to heal that pain of separation. So many people that I have encountered in my work seem to experience that state of disconnection to their lives here. Alienated from others through their silences, unable to communicate their deepest feelings and needs, many of them are still, metaphorically, in that bardo state. Out of touch with their bodies, they drift along, seemingly unable to connect with where the meaning lies in their life. It takes bravery to take those first steps, to risk being vulnerable. It is worth remembering, that if we protect ourselves from being vulnerable, from taking risks and maybe getting hurt sometimes, we are simply 'staying safe' and not growing. Spiritual development comes from facing challenges, learning lessons and developing qualities like resilience and courage in the process as we come to a place of understanding in ourselves.

We are never alone, they are always with us.

PERSONAL NOTES

Enlightenment

SECTION 6

SPIRITUAL DEVELOPMENT

CHAPTER 19
Jilly's story

It is always exciting to work with those people who ask for past life regression as a part of their spiritual development. Often these individuals are experienced meditators and are able to go into deep states of trance quite easily. Jilly was one of those rare individuals to whom the trance state is quite natural, and I had the privilege of working with her on a regular basis with past life regression work for three years. Her first experience was a momentous one for both of us when she spontaneously relived her own birth. She had come in with issues around her throat, and an almost paralysing sense of feeling 'stuck' in her life. Often, she told me, she felt a strong desire to speak in another language that she did not recognise. After encouraging her to do so if she felt the impulse, I induced her very easily using her own meditation process as an induction, then instructed her to go to the source of her current difficulties, knowing that her subconscious would take her where she needed to go.

"Dark dome shape – flickering light…very deep…almost like into a tunnel...hole. Can't see end…I'm going into a vacuum." Her voice is very quiet, almost a whisper, and I lean forward to hear her better. She is quiet for about five minutes, then, wondering where she is in her process, I ask her:
"Can you let yourself go in?"
"It's getting lighter…feel something on my face…light is coming. Feel just floaty, pleasant, becoming lighter. Something thick on my face, around my nostrils, near my mouth, feels heavy but OK."
"How old are you?" I ask.
"No sense of age – arms feel really heavy, left one feels like a dead weight – tingly, hand feels tingly. Feel arm more now, it's numb." She seems stuck and I encourage her to move if she needs to.
"Let the feeling take you deeper into the experience."
"Feeling is going into my legs now, now into middle finger of left hand. She stretches and tells me "Stretching releases the energy." She wriggles around for a while, seemingly enjoying the movement.
"Go to the feeling in your throat now," I say as she turns onto her side, asking if it is OK.
"Yes you can turn onto your side and still remain in a very relaxed state."
"See light …bits of light," she says suddenly. "I am in a deep space, don't want to move."
"You can stay there until you want to move," I confirm. (At this point I have a strong intuition that she needs to be aware of her decision to move and leave her there in the space for some time until she is ready).
"The light is coming, tunnel is opening up. There is half a dome of light now. It is nice, I am floating."
"Allow the light to come," I encourage her.
"Feel safe for some reason – have made a decision to be there. Beams of light coming from above now …like rays of sun." She is quiet for some time, and, wondering whether to speak or not, I wait for a while before asking her:
"What do you feel in your body?"
"Peaceful," she replies.
"You can be comfortable lying there and know when you need to move," I reassure her.
Some time elapses before she says suddenly, "I feel like bursting forth."
"Just let yourself do that now, it is quite safe, it is your decision," I remind her.

She begins to breathe more quickly, panting, alternating with long slow breaths and I am in awe, realising that I am watching her actual rebirthing. "I am in a lighter brighter area, feel distant to my body – energy in my arms and wrists."

"Can you see your body now?" I ask her in wonder.

" Just light… happy to be where I am, body feels very weighted, hands feel pinned, almost like being held down."

She stays there for quite a while in this space before indicating that she is ready to be brought back, elated by her experience, and very relaxed.

The lesson here appeared to be very clearly about Jilly making the decision to move rather than having the decision made for her. On discussion, she felt strongly that it could relate to the fact that she was induced at birth. From my perspective as a facilitator, this experience was very like the birth process, and I marvelled at what a difference it seemed to make to her, to be able to go back and make the decision, like Annie, to be here in this lifetime. As an induced baby myself, I could well understand the reluctance to be dragged out clasped by a pair of cold metal forceps into the harsh brightness and noise of a delivery room.

Jilly became fascinated by the regression process and found it so beneficial for her wellbeing that she went on to have regular sessions for three years. After the first few sessions, she trusted me enough to verbalise the strange words and sounds that were 'caught' in her throat. It sounded like a different language, however, although we tried on several occasions to tape it, her voice was so soft that it was impossible to pick up anything clearly enough in the recording. This phenomenon is known as xenoglossia.

Several of her regressions took her to India and she was very interested to know if what she was speaking was an ancient Hindu dialect as she believed. I transcribed phonetically as best I could from what I was hearing and we were eventually able to identify some words which appeared to be contextually accurate. For example, in one regression when she was experiencing something that was distressing for her, she called out the same word over and over several times. Later investigations identified it as the Hindu word for 'help'.

Jilly experienced many lifetimes in India, several with her current family members in different types of relationships. Always, the main theme was her spiritual development and each lifetime seemed to build on the experiences of the previous one. She was a very wise, compassionate soul. On follow up, Jilly had this to say about her experiences.

"When reflecting upon the impact of my regression sessions with Val, I had many thoughts running through my brain but I found it very hard to articulate them into words. Luckily, I found my journal that contained my experiences of each session. Whilst reading the whole journal, I found it took me back through a very special journey Val and I had shared together. It brought up my memory of how comfortable I felt with her. She created an environment that felt so safe, nurturing and healing as we shared the journey together. When I came to reading the very last session, I realised it summed up everything I was trying to articulate in a nutshell. I have come to a place of healing, restoration, knowledge and truth. I have explored what I have needed to explore, gone to the core and explored the knowledge within. It's like coming to the core of the earth and connecting with our essential true nature. Truth and Knowledge keeps coming up; how important it is to get in touch with our inner core and then all is healed.'

The journey that I took with Jilly taught me as much as it did her, and I will always be grateful to her too for trusting me enough to go there with me.

CHAPTER 20
Ruth's story

Ruth had previously had a regression and found it very comforting in confirming her spiritual path. I had known her for some time as a fellow professional and she told me that she had initially sought me out because of the spiritual orientation that I brought to my work, which was very pleasing. She was eager to try another to see if she could access more information. Separated from her husband for some time, she was finding her way as a single parent and wondering if she would ever meet the soul mate that she knew was waiting for her.

Now familiar with the process, she relaxed very quickly into a deep state of trance and went straight to a childhood memory.

"I'm lying in a paddock, lush green grass, looking up in the sky, being in nature…I feel sad." She is silent for a while.

"What is your sadness about?" I ask her, curious about her mood in such pleasant surroundings.

"I feel happy in nature but alone in the world." She speaks softly and I lean closer to hear her better.

This often happens in regressions; some people actually see their story like a movie and the speaking of it is often an effort as multiple images present themselves in quick succession. With these very hypnotic clients, I try to keep questions to a minimum to avoid disrupting their own process.

"I'm 13…14 years old, by myself…wearing white tank top, red things on it, and shorts. Don't feel good about myself," she frowns and quickly goes to another memory. "Blue bike, I'm with my brother, we play outside together. Playing… not thinking," she adds emphatically, and I know she is trying to tell me this is important.

"What are you meant to learn from these experiences?" I ask her.

"To be happy, joyful," she responds and then quickly her expression changes as she moves immediately to another memory. "Old haggard woman, like a witch, I look grotesque!" she grimaces. "Feel like a witch, old and nasty, grumpy and mean. No one wants to be around me…I have created it that way…body floating, elevated. There's a man, I know him… from his eyes. He's gone again," she cries softly. "I'm floating…we want contact…it's not allowed or right… his eyes…get lost in them. I know him, so much love and connection." Tears stream down her face. She stretches out her arms. "He's taking my hand and kissing it. He doesn't speak to me, just looks at me. I've known him some time… joy…he knows me, I know him. We were together once, I think I long for that."

"Go back to that time," I instruct her.

"There was some reason…war…we were together. I don't know why we were separated." She is still distressed, and thinking to help her I say;

"You can allow yourself to find that joy again. Release the pain of this separation."

"I feel empty without him." She is unable to let go. "He's telling me he will be OK, but he doesn't have to live with it…his eyes are saying it's ok." She is quiet for a while.

"What happens to you?" I probe eventually, after a period of silence.

"I'm floating again…lights around me, healing me."

"Take in the healing," I urge her.

"I know we will be together again," she says quietly after some time has passed in silence. She seems peaceful now.

"You will know when he's here," I tell her, *"you will recognise him by his eyes."*

Ruth is a beautiful young woman, both inside and out; I know how long she has waited for this special person to come into her life and feel sure that she will find love again.

"I'm not worried now," she says confidently, "just trust…must have faith. I'm on the right track. All is as it should be."

"Yes." *I confirm it for her, "just trust, know you are on the right path."*

"Keep getting Steve (ex partner) is going away…his decision," she adds.

"Can you be comfortable with this now?" I ask her.

"Yes. See me older…smart woman, something to say about her work…but not more important than other things. My passion…I have much to give and share. My work will take me far and wide and my path will be laid out for me. All I need is to walk along it. I will know when I start resisting that I need to trust it. He will be my shining light in this World-a great person…lots of good times with me." Her eyes are flickering rapidly under her eyelids and I know she is processing a lot of information. "We will help each other."

"You can see your future together, and you can go on with your own life in the meantime." I confirm it for her, not wanting her to be in limbo until he arrives.

"It's all right, it's already been written, we are all connected." Her voice is confident, sure. "Just let go and be." She is telling me now. "Enjoy where you are, because this is all part of it too. I will be happy-life will give me everything I hoped. I can speak in tongues, different language tones…they are speaking to me differently, speak through me." Her face glows with happiness and I leave her in the space to enjoy these feelings, leaving her to return when she is ready. It is always a privilege to work with individuals like this, who have done their own personal growth work and who are committed to their own spiritual path, wherever it may take them. Ruth came for several regressions and her spiritual development was very apparent through them.

On the third visit, Ruth was eager to continue and able to move very quickly into a trance state, as evidenced by the rapid flickering of her eyelids.

"I'm in a tunnel of light…new…it's Atlantis. I'm flying above it, looking down on islands; up high in the sky…misty…cloud cover…can see through it. Connected to vision of this man…good connection…we have a love connection. Not sure why I'm up here."

"Allow the energy to take you where you need to go," I direct her.

She is quiet for a while, frowning, and I wait for her to resolve the dilemma herself.

"I'm conflicted, I want to go but connection to him is holding me. I'm turning away-its ok. He needs me but I know he will be ok. We will meet again. When we do, it will be like there was never lifetimes between us. I feel I have that connection now…feel it again. Don't know why I want to go there, it's in my heart, totally unconditional, like a beautiful rose. Heart is open…amazing being this open." Her face reflects her wonder. "See him but don't see him…feel him. Haven't felt this for a long time…no need to worry-yet I have. Our lives have always been entwined." She seems to be gathering information, and, curious about the source I ask her:

"How is the energy around you?"

She continues as though she hasn't heard me – she is deeply immersed in the story and the question is not relevant for her. "I'm stable in my life, content, not in a hurry. He needs me…going through things…send love to him…reassurance…will connect again when it is time. Connect through the heart…this is how we used to connect. Heart's just a beacon…sends waves of energy out. This is how we will connect again as humans…through the heart."

Her expression changes and she moves restlessly. "Changed again now…don't feel so open…go with energy flow." It appears as though she is still accessing information from another source and I wait for her to speak when she is ready, not wanting to interrupt her processing. It is always a fine line, when to ask a question which has the potential to lead her in an entirely different direction. This is one of the main problems with the way some past life regressions are conducted, the person is 'led' in a particular direction by the questioning of the facilitator, which can be more about what they 'see' or want to know than the individual's own process.

Eventually she sighs. "In my life now something prevents me…don't do it much…not fear, fear of what that will mean. My life's going to change in lots of ways, not sure how…fear…like a cloak. Every time I try and open cloak up, it's just there. Just trust…shifted now…light on path of protection. Time to make a movement, ready to walk down that path…its ok. Can see a lot of joy. Can see myself very joyful, family around me, lots of laughter." She is smiling, and I affirm it for her.

"It's ok for you to be happy now."

"Important for me not to fear and to trust…trust my feelings. Just speak from that place. Can trust yourself to know what's right for you…no more pain…no karmic pain…it will be lighter and easier. You can be free." She repeats what she is being told.

"Experiencing heart really open, rest of body really heavy. Heart is eternal, can tune into this energy. Child in me is dancing with joy. Child is happy that I recognize that now."

"You will be all right. She knows that you will look after her, she trusts you now." I re affirm it for her.

"It's about being connected to everything…nature," she continues. "Can still protect self with bubble whenever need to. Joy… also I'm getting time…always exactly right time. We can be scared if something comes to us, trust that time is right for us to have it. Also about letting go of others."

"They have their own journeys," I agree.

"Yes…just want to help them more. I just go… past life when I was a gypsy…fortune teller. Promise myself I would lead this life that I am leading now, or just coming into. Keep my promise to myself-I remember that promise now. I'm just wondering about the man, why it's so important…unconditional love."

"Is he known to you in your current life?" I ask her.

"No… will know when I meet him…when time is right…nothing you need to do. When time is right…it will happen." There seems nothing more and I bring her back.

"Allow yourself to gently drop back to earth as your body gets heavier."

"My heart is still light and open."

Following the regression she seems content and happy. Each regression experience moved her forward in her life and confirmed something for her; each story part of a larger story, the journey of her spiritual development. Ruth returned for regular sessions and it was a delight to see her progress rapidly in her professional development as well as on her spiritual path. The regressions gave her confidence in herself and her abilities and she was able to deal with the painful times with grace and acceptance, knowing that she would be happy again. Knowing that the pain would pass, gave her hope for her future happiness.

It was a privilege to witness the unfolding of her soul's purpose and the healing that it brought to her.

CHAPTER 21
Andrew's story

Andrew wanted to experience a past life regression mainly out of interest, but he was also hoping to gain some clarity about his life's purpose. Often I find that those who have chosen to explore their spiritual purpose through regression, already seem to be on the right path, but just need that little extra bit of clarification to trust it. So it was with Andrew. The clues were there already in his life, but the regression served to clarify it for him.

It took some time to relax him as he was very 'cognitive' in his approach. Analysing information and making sense of it was second nature to him, and I suspected that he was left hemisphere dominant. This simply means that his brain favoured a structured, analytical approach rather than the more emotional, intuitive function of the right hemisphere. With individuals like this, it is important to take an approach which encourages them out of their thinking function into their feelings.

After massaging his third eye to encourage visualisation, we spent some time contracting and expanding his body awareness before flying around over the rooftops (you would be amazed at what people see up there!) Soon, Andrew indicated that he was ready to begin regressing back and quickly went to a childhood memory.

"I'm swimming…at school…big wall… cracked pieces of concrete, have to be careful where I step, might hurt my toe. I'm 7 or 8. It's a good day…I get to swim… It's a swimming test… to see if I am ready for swimming in deep water. Good feeling." Already my antennae are going up with this metaphorical reference to being in deep water, but as he is impatient to move on, I make a mental note of it before regressing him back further.

His next memory is of being 4 or 5. "See white nurse's hat," he tells me, "on the table, bottom of the stairs; I got in trouble for something. I'm very young. Hat is white with folds, Mum is very protective of the hat-it is hers. She had to make the folds. Got in trouble a lot… wasn't good," he reflected. At this point his conscious mind takes control as he remarks that he can't see the relevance of all this.

"Just trust the process," I tell him before taking him down some steps to try and deepen his state.

The more relaxed a person is, the easier it is for the subconscious to come to the fore. Finally, we reach what appears to be a past life memory and his body goes very still as though he is watching something.

"I'm outside a building…looking at it," he confirms. "Square, don't recognise it, somewhere in Europe? Central door, sandy coloured, shades under the roof at the front. Like a court house, government building. I'm looking at it; know I have to go in…steps at front of building." There is a longish pause while he contemplates. Wanting to avoid his conscious mind going into analytical mode, I encourage him;

"Do you want to go in?"

"Yes." He duly goes in and begins to report back. "Wide open space, stairway to left…white with tall roof. I have an appointment." He pauses again and begins to fidget. Firmly, I bring him back to the moment, knowing that at this early stage, it is easy for him to come back out of trance.

"Allow it to progress as it will."

His body relaxes again. "I'm talking to the receptionist; I'm a male, aged maybe 30's. Older clothes, strange colour, brown…brown trousers, waistcoat, smart shoes. The appointment is important to me, I'm being tested. (My antennae go up again!) I have an idea, theory…something. They are asking me questions." He turns his head as though listening and then frowns suddenly. "I feel a sense of anger with them, they're blind, they don't see." He struggles to articulate his theory and I give him a suggestion that it will now become clear to him.

"Organising people, the way something should be run…it's a new approach. They don't value them…makes me angry. People have no idea, they only see themselves, they don't really care." He sounds bitter and continues on, his voice rising with the perceived injustice of it. "They listen; they understand but still don't change." I wonder if he is talking about himself and attempt to get some clarification.

"Why is that?"

"It takes their power away from them."

"Who are they?"

"Leaders, officials," he says dismissively. "I am only discussing with one man." There is another period of contemplation and I remain quiet, wanting him to decide when to move on. "They are scared," he tells me finally. "They understand my theory but they don't like to change. They can't help me. I'm not angry for long," he pauses, before exclaiming in excitement. "He writes! He returns to the sea…I see waves."

"Do you know his name?"

"I get Alfred."

"What is the purpose of this life?"

"Communicating. Reflecting on the life we discussed-had to share something, but people didn't listen."

"What is the lesson here?" I encourage him to understand the relevance.

"To change people's perspective, they think I didn't do enough."

"What more did they want you to do?"

"They wanted me to have more of an impact."

"Your purpose…this is what you are meant to do?"

"I often lack motivation," he admits finally.

"What will help you achieve what you want?"

"Self belief. I don't believe it to be true. My belief being tested," he realises. "Things I'm meant to do…There's a group of people…seen them before, maybe the same…in a dream?"

"Can you describe them?" I'm wondering if this is his spiritual guides.

"They see right through me. I feel this is a group I belong to. They are objective, hard."

"They are always there?"

"They are there to oversee my progress…I'm doing OK…it hasn't been easy…pain. They tell me I'm more than I think."

"What is their message to you?"

"Wake up and go! They will see me soon. They allow me to go back. They give me a state…a feeling from which I can communicate with them. Use light within to be balanced. The vortex is the connection between me and them. My partner…is in the same group! It doesn't matter-there are more lifetimes…it's ok…it's just one more lifetime."

He sounds relieved. Finally he has got it; he knows what he must do. When he wakens fully, we discuss the possible lessons that have come out of these experiences.

"I have to believe in myself," he says confidently. "I'm being tested to see if I'm ready for deep water."

I have to smile, yet when I refer to his early memory of the childhood swimming test, he doesn't get the connection straight away. I love how the subconscious often supplies the clues in double meanings and metaphors! It's such a fascinating process to be a party to.

"Wake up and go!" they tell him. "Write the book!"

"I can connect with them via the vortex…there are more lifetimes than this one," he explains to me and leaves happily, a little bemused by his experience. I am pleased for him that he got the clarity he was seeking and look forward to seeing his book in print.

CHAPTER 22
Sarah's story

Sarah's life story was a fascinating one. The only child of her adoring parents, she had experienced a magical childhood as a young girl. Happy and sunny, she was the centre of their world until the war intervened to turn her world upside down. Coming from a Jewish background, she found herself suddenly uprooted and sent away for her own safety. Here is her story.

"I'm on the train…a young girl, about 2 years old…feel upset," (she begins to cry softly). "I don't know where I am…don't know where my parents are. Lots of big kids there…frightened…overwhelmed, don't know what to do. In Wales? Don't know…my arm hurts. Don't know if I will ever see my parents again. Didn't like it there, all alone…no way out…not big enough to do anything. Trapped…fear…left in the dark not understanding. Feels like I'm disintegrating, going into millions of pieces…annihilation…fear of it…black hole…tunnel. Unreal…nowhere…feels like I'm by myself."

I could only begin to imagine the absolute terror that she must have felt, torn away from the safe, protected environment that she was used to and then finding herself without her family, amidst many other equally frightened little souls. Then, suddenly, she is floating, at peace.

"It doesn't matter any more…nothing there…I'm floating inside something…black…feels like an oval…domed…water…uterus? Very comfortable, warm and quiet, safe…nothing can get me."

"Do you have a sense of your self?"

"Doesn't feel as solid as this body. Have a shape, not as much weight, without features." She is silent for a while.

"Can you move forward a little and see what happens to you"?

"I'm in the womb…nice place to be…safe and warm. I'd like to stay there," she tells me. I leave her there for a while and then, wanting to bring her to the time of the contract she made for this lifetime, I say,

"Go to a time when you can't stay there."

"Annoyed…angry…I don't want to move…no say in it. What I want doesn't matter, it's going to happen, I don't have a say. Have to do what somebody else wants to do, not what I want – don't know what's going to happen. I'm helpless, caught in it again, like a fly in a spider's web, like to get out, feel stuck."

I sense that there is something here about the baby or the mother making a decision and leave her to make sense of it.

She sighs eventually. "It's a process beyond my control. I don't know what's going to happen."

"What is the lesson you are meant to learn?"

"Acceptance." I note that she doesn't sound convinced.

"Is there anything else you could do?" I wonder.

"No. There's no way around it." She is resigned to the reality of her birth, not believing that she had a choice in it. I can see where she might be stuck in her thinking, she does not believe that she made a choice to come here, to this lifetime, I remember her telling me during her first session, that all her life, people had made decisions for her. The feeling of powerlessness plays out in her life again and again; she is unable to manifest the things that she wants.

"Why is this unfair?" I ask her.

"Don't know. Can't get my own way."

"What do you need to do to resolve this?"
She is quiet for a while, reflective, then, "I could adjust my thinking, if I have made the choice, it's ok," she muses, "if it's beyond my control, I have to make the most of the situation. I have to decide what I want to experience." Finally, she is able to see some options.

"I do have a choice!" she realises. "It's just two sides of the same coin – two different learning's. I'm not stuck - it's me who has the choice!" She is thrilled by this new understanding and goes on to explain.

"The good things are the patience, wisdom and knowledge to be gained by being there. The bad things are the angry, resentful feelings. I can accept both of these, knowing it's all for my own learning."

I am pleased for her that she has found some resolution, and she leaves happily after making an appointment for another session.

Next session, she is eager to continue the exploration. She easily recalls two early childhood memories before going to the time between lives, when the contract was made for her to come here.

"See a pointy stone thing…gravestone?" She wonders aloud. Then, "there's a face trying to come through. In his 50's…60's? There's an impression of sternness, unapproachable. Stone of the grave is hard, there's writing on it…a border…straight line…words stand out. Somebody lying down…man's face. Long time ago, ancient teacher, respected, rigid. Sandals, long dress, outfit creamy grey soft material." Immediately, I think of a monk or a druid but say nothing, waiting for her to continue.

"Beard, broad forehead-alive now."

(I presume she means that she is seeing the man from the grave before he dies).

"Sense a young boy, 15 or 16 years old. Place of stone edifices, might be a lecture place, place of learning," she tells me. He's a teacher, very knowledgeable, it's a long time ago. He's not a relaxed person. Very well educated, focussed on intellectual pursuits. Has kept his focus very closed-has chosen formal academic way of doing things. In his late 50's," she confirms. "He is stuck. His purpose is to teach, but he's very dry, capable but intellectual….enclosed around him, restricted. He's allowing it to happen, knows this stuff has got his students, could learn a lot, facts, but he's not stimulating." She can see how he is failing in his approach to engage his students. They respect him but don't really listen."

I ask her to move forward in his life to find out what happens to him.

"Greece. More sunshine, open," she says immediately. He's there but not teaching, he's freer, dryness is gone. "Is he happy now?" I ask her.

"Yes," she says simply. "Different feeling now, felt closed, dead, dry, like stone. Now he has colour, life. Dark hair – younger?" she wonders aloud. "Staff in his hand, dressed in brown, creamy wrap thing, has life and energy – the other part of him." I wonder if she is seeing an earlier lifetime for this man and ask her about the lessons that he is supposed to learn.

"He is entering into life, not just talking about it. Healthy, fun person, strong voice, does things, doesn't just talk about things."

"What is his contract in this life?"

"He is a leader with his people, not respected like a lecturer. One of the people, gets really into life, with his hands- gets physically involved, other one intellectually involved." She is eager that I understand the difference in the two men. "He can put his knowledge to use in a very practical way, vitality in his blood. Get in there to where the people are," she emphasises. "He doesn't get caught up in academia, gets involved in the world. His presence makes a difference," she says simply. I know that this is what she wants too, to make a difference with her work. Her final comment

sums up the difference for her. "I see him not attached to anything. Doesn't belong to any body of learning, he is independent of it, has enough strength to do that.
This man is able to give them some of his strength, he can help them."

She seems to be struggling with a dichotomy; two types of leader, both with different styles. One appears bound by bureaucracy, the other, a man of the people. Later in her regression work, she describes seeing rich archetypal symbols which she incorporates into her artwork. Afterwards, I reflect on how she has often complained of feeling hemmed in by bureaucracy, unable to achieve what she wants for herself, and hope that this helps her to move forward in her chosen field. She leaves happily, with more of a sense of ownership of her life.

CHAPTER 23
Bluebirds

This story begins in the 1960's when I was at High school in Bristol, in the south west of England. I met a girl there whom I instantly connected with. Judith subsequently became my best friend and had a very profound influence on my life not only during those teenage years, but for many years afterwards. She taught me, by example, how to give of your very best in everything that you do. She also loved me unconditionally and that was the first time in my life that I had felt that.

I suppose we were both oddballs in our own way. During our formative years, we were more interested in looking after Thumper and Joker, the school's pet rabbits than boys, and spent many a cold winter's day during the holidays, trudging the two miles through the snow to feed them and let them out for a run. Judith was the daughter of a police inspector and we had many exciting escapades, notably riding in the back of the paddy wagon one night when her dad had a call out while he was coming to pick us up from Guides. We didn't get home until late after unloading our burglar at the police station and by that time, both mothers were distraught with worry.

When Judith's father was transferred back to the country during our last two senior years in High school, we were both devastated. I don't know to this day why we lost contact, but, sadly, we did. Several years later I followed a boyfriend to Australia and never returned, but I never forgot her or our time together. About two years ago, I decided to try and find her again and wrote to my mother asking if she could send her address. To my everlasting sorrow, Mum told me that Judith had died of cancer a couple of years earlier. How bitterly I regretted not having made the effort to keep in contact with her.

I had a strong compulsion to write to her parents, despite being advised by Mum and Dad not to as they thought it would cause them too much pain to hear from me so soon after her death. I left it another year and then wrote, telling them of the profound influence she had on my life. Judith always got top marks for all her assignments and tests - she had a brilliant mind. I did my very best to emulate her and usually ended up with 9 1/2 out of ten while she of course, got 10. In that, she taught me to do the very best that you are capable of.

Her Mum wrote back to tell me that they were so thrilled to get my letter and wanted me to know that Judith had loved me and cherished our friendship. She said that my parents and I had opened a new door in her life and sent me a photo of her with their next letter, taken just before she was diagnosed with cancer. It was wonderful to see how she looked as she matured, with the same beautiful smile and warmth in her eyes that I remembered.

That same night, I had an unusually vivid experience. Whilst in that semi conscious state just before sleep, I 'saw' Judith in a long blue nurses uniform with a sort of mantle around her head, like a nun's, and a red cross on the front. The words 'French military field hospital…first world war …and La Sorbonne' came to me quite clearly and I could see Judith smiling at me, as though she was trying to tell me something. It was so different to a dream, almost three dimensional in quality as though she was actually there. I have had these flashes before and it is almost like tuning in to a different channel on a television.

It was so vivid that I woke up determined to do some research and told my friend Charlotte about it who immediately jumped on the internet and typed in the words that had come to me. After looking at many extracts and pictures of the nurses uniforms of that period I was disappointed not to be able to find anything that resembled what I had seen. Luckily for me, Charlotte was not ready to let go of the trail. Her persistence led us to a very small entry about the Red Cross. "Could it have been the Red Cross rather than a nurse's uniform?" she asked. Instantly, I knew that it was, and when a picture came up of a woman wearing exactly what I had seen, I was thrilled.

Before she let me read the extract, Charlotte asked me whether I felt that my ability with the French language was because I had been born there at some time, or just learned it previously. The only exposure I have had to the language was when I took the subject at High school some forty years ago; however, to this day, I can still speak conversational French, albeit rusty. (On one of my visits home some years ago, I took my mum to Paris, something I had always been drawn to do). I was very definite that I had been taught the language rather than being born there, not feeling 'fluent' as a native French person would. Charlotte then showed me the photograph of the 'Bluebirds'-a group of twenty Australian women who had volunteered for the Red Cross during the 1st world war together with their French teacher who went along to assist them with the language.
"You have bluebirds all over your house!" she exclaimed. I became very emotional at hearing the name Bluebirds and knew they were connected with the uniform I had seen which I intuitively felt was made of a heavy blue serge. You can imagine how amazed I was to see the photograph of two of the nurses with their pet rabbit, which looked just like the one Judith used to look after at school. I was even more intrigued to read that the nurses were often sent off in pairs to the various places which had been converted into temporary hospitals and was certain that Judith had been my partner.

This story becomes even more startling. The very next day after I returned home to the south west, Charlotte rang me to tell me that her friend Kate, who was camping in the bush, had rung her that day to tell her that she was seeing bluebirds everywhere and had just gone back to bury one that she had found dead on the side of the road. She wanted to know if Charlotte knew what bluebirds symbolised and was amazed to hear about my story.

It gets odder. At the same time, Kate had met a group of women while she was away and was very keen for Charlotte to meet them. They subsequently were invited to dinner where they met a young woman called Jo. When Charlotte heard them talking about France and a chateau, which I think may have been converted to a hospital during the first world war, her ears pricked up immediately as you can imagine. We were both stunned to find out that her mother was one of the original Bluebirds.

Initially, I was not sure what to make of all this. The synchronicities are too many to be attributable to pure chance. I have always hated war movies and television shows about medical procedures, not because I am 'squeamish' but because there is that strange feeling that I have seen enough of that before. I have always liked clothing with piping and I believe that the Bluebirds uniform had blue piping around the edges of their uniforms - and I love bluebirds! I wonder whether Judith and I had a past life together as Bluebirds, but given that we were both born around 1949, that would mean that we would have to have 'died' before then to be reborn now.

Whatever the truth may be, I am certain that it was Judith's way of letting me know that there are more lives than this one and that we had been together before and will be again. It enabled me to let go of the sorrow of our lost contact, knowing that this life is just a blink of an eye in the fabric of time.

Summary

This book was not written to prove the existence of past lives, or even to provide a philosophical basis for understanding them. It is no easy matter to find incontrovertible proof; even Stevenson's exhaustive attempts to validate children's past life experiences in India and Turkey have had doubts cast upon them by others who suggest that prior conditioning to the existence of reincarnation may have influenced their receptivity to the concept. However, there have also been many accounts of clients discovering historically accurate details and images which they believe confirm their own experience.

The research into past lives has already been extensively covered by Roger Woolger in his excellent work 'Other Lives, Other Selves – A Jungian Psychotherapist Discovers Past Lives,' which offers a comprehensive review and summary of the area. Those readers who wish to know more about the background and philosophical approaches which underpin the theory will doubtless enjoy his comprehensive and well written book. At the time it was written, in the 1980's, past life therapy was still a relatively new therapeutic approach. Now there are numerous modalities which claim success in retrieving past life memories. Having said that, I am a firm believer that this type of therapy should only be undertaken by those who have received professional training in the field of psychology, not because I believe psychologists or psychiatrists are the only people who can do this work. On the contrary, there are many ways of accessing the unconscious; the danger is that in unleashing such memories, the person may not have sufficient ego strength to deal with them, and this is where the support of a professional who is trained to assess an individual's mental state and work with the emotions that are released is so vital. I know that Brian Weiss, my mentor, also supports this view. I refer the reader to the many books that he has written on the subject of regression in recommended reading.

My aim in sharing these stories is that it will give people hope that there is a reality other than the one that we experience on a daily basis. We are spiritual beings having a human experience and to know that there is a point to our experiences, that we are here to learn lessons from which we can progress spiritually can be very comforting, particularly during difficult times in our lives.

A close friend of mine, who died at 33 years of age of a brain tumour, had several experiences of trauma to the head during her past lives. In one, she was a commander of an army who was shot in the back of the head while standing outside an underground bunker in which her men were hiding from the enemy. She described in detail the grey uniform and headgear that she was wearing and was able to identify them later from pictures as those worn by a Turkish commander several hundred years previously. Typically, she felt responsible for the welfare of her men and suffered massive guilt about her inability to prevent their deaths. In this lifetime, she had been a strong advocate and tireless worker in the area of youth suicide prevention, often 'butting heads' as she liked to call it, with those organisations whose policies she saw as failing dismally to meet the needs of young people at risk.

In an earlier lifetime as a primitive tribe dweller, she was eaten by a bear while running away, the main injury being to the back of her head where the bear had grasped her in its jaws. Yet, despite her deep spiritual awareness and understanding of why she had developed tumours in this very area, she seemed unable to let go of the unrelenting anger that drove her to do so much good work in this life. Her intimate relationships were fraught with conflict as she demanded much from them and those who failed to meet her expectations bore the brunt of her wrath. However, the regressions offered her some comfort, to know that there was a point to all the suffering, and that there would be other opportunities for her to let it go. As she was dying, she said to me, "my body is very heavy, but my spirit is strong." If she were still here, I am sure she would be pointing out that this was her karma, to die for a cause worth dying for, perhaps to make amends for a previous lifetime.

The other reason that motivated me to write this book was to let people know that they do not have to suffer the agonising physical and emotional distress that many of them carry around on a daily basis. Even just one regression can have a profoundly healing effect as evidenced by some of these uplifting stories. Guilt can spontaneously disappear as understanding takes its place and, in some cases, chronic physical symptoms can be eased or disappear spontaneously. Strangely enough, even when the individual does not believe in reincarnation the positive effects occur. It's as though our guides and helpers are just waiting for an opportunity to help us heal – we just have to ask.

From my perspective, writing this book has brought me more rewards than I could have imagined. Apart from helping me to fulfil my soul's purpose, it has enabled me to receive feedback from the many people that I have helped with this work, and that is a joy, to know that I have in some small way contributed to their wellbeing and the health of our beautiful planet. In the words of George Bernard Shaw;

"This is the true joy in life, the being used for a purpose recognised by yourself as a mighty one; the being a force of nature instead of a feverish, selfish little clod of ailments and grievances, complaining that the world will not devote itself to making you happy.

I am of the opinion that my life belongs to the whole community, and as long as I live it is my privilege to do for it whatever I can.

I want to be thoroughly used up when I die, for the harder I work, the more I live. I rejoice in life for its own sake. Life is no brief candle to me; it is a sort of splendid torch which I have got hold of for the moment, and I want to make it burn as brightly as possible before handing it on to future generations."

Blessed Be

Valarie

Enquiries and feedback via my email vcoventry@bigpond.com are welcome.

Author profile

Valarie is a fully qualified psychologist and hypnotherapist who lives and works in the beautiful state of Western Australia.

Her passion is in helping people heal through a combination of counseling and hypnotherapy. She has a particular interest in regression therapy which uses hypnosis to uncover spiritual lessons and blocks to progress in this lifetime.

She travelled all the way to America to train with Brian Weiss, one of the World's leading regression therapists and author of several life changing books including 'Many Lives, Many Masters' and 'Through Time into Healing". Later, she followed this up with a diploma in Hypnotherapy from the Milton Erickson Institute in WA. This enabled her to broaden the application of her hypnotherapy work to include the use of hypnosis for health and lifestyle goals.

Valarie's deep commitment to healing, both at an individual and planetary level, is reflected in her private psychology practices in Perth and Bunbury, her artwork and her teaching.

All artwork in the book, with the exception of the cover design, is by Valarie.

To contact Valarie, email vcoventry@bigpond.com or visit her blog
www.yoursouliscallingyou.blogspot.com.au

Hypnotherapy Soul Journeys

By
Valarie Coventry
B App. Sc (Psychology)
Dip. Hypnotherapy

Love Yourself & Be Happy

A safe and enjoyable way to access the power of your own mind and achieve your goals through self hypnosis.

Copyright © 2010 • Valarie Coventry • All rights reserved

Hypnotherapy Soul Journeys

By
Valarie Coventry
B App. Sc (Psychology)
Dip Hypnotherapy

CD
Time: 27min

Love Yourself & Be Happy

A safe and enjoyable way to access the power of your own mind and achieve your goals through self hypnosis.

Hypnotherapy Soul Journeys

By
Valarie Coventry
B App. Sc (Psychology)
Dip. Hypnotherapy

Heal Yourself & Be Well

A safe and enjoyable way to access the power of your own mind and achieve your goals through self hypnosis.

Copyright © 2011   •   Valarie Coventry   •   All rights reserved

Hypnotherapy Soul Journeys

By
Valarie Coventry
B App. Sc (Psychology)
Dip Hypnotherapy

CD
Time: 27min

Heal Yourself & Be Well

A safe and enjoyable way to access the power of your own mind and achieve your goals through self hypnosis.

Recommended reading

These are the books that have most informed and influenced me. There are many others, so be guided by your own intuition in your reading.

Regression stories
Brian Weiss
Many Lives, Many Masters
Through Time into Healing
Only Love is Real
Messages from the Masters
Same Soul, Many Bodies

Sylvia Brown – Past Lives, Future Healing
B Goldberg – Past Lives, Future Lives
J Iverson – More Lives Than One

Research and Philosophical approaches to Past Life regression
Roger Woolger - Other Lives, Other Selves-A Jungian Psychotherapist Discovers Past Lives
G.M. Glaskin – The Christos Experience: Windows of the Mind

The Afterlife
Raymond Moody -Life Between Lives
Helen Greaves-Testimony of Light: An extraordinary message of life after death.
P Berman-The Journey Home: What near death experiences and mysticism teach us about the gift of Life.
J L Whitton & J Fisher - Life Between Life
Kevin J Todeschi – Edgar Cayce on the Akashic Records

Spiritual Development
Caroline Myss
Anatomy of the Spirit
The Creation of Health
Sacred Contracts

Karmic pathway references
Gary Goldschneider & Joost Elffers
The Secret Language of Destiny: A personology guide to finding your life purpose.

Mark's book – visit www.frogandthewell.com